# TWO PHILOSOPHERS WRESTLE WITH
# GOD

## A DIALOGUE

By Dr. Jerry L. Martin and
Dr. Richard Oxenberg

Two Philosophers Wrestle with God: A Dialogue
Copyright © 2024 Jerry L. Martin and Richard Oxenberg
Caladium Publishing Company, LLC
Doylestown, PA

Aside from brief passages in a published review, no part of this book may be reproduced or transmitted in any form or by any means, electronic or mechanical, including all technologies known or later developed, without written permission from the publisher.

www.caladiumpublishing.com

For media inquiries and requests, please contact
Jerry L. Martin at
Jerry.martin@godanautobiography.com

ISBN: 978-0-9967253-4-7 (Paperback edition)
ISBN: 978-0-9967253-5-4 (Ebook edition)

Layout and Design by Integrative Ink

# TWO PHILOSOPHERS WRESTLE WITH
# GOD

## A DIALOGUE

# Table of Contents

*Acknowledgments* ............................................................. vii
*Foreword - By Jerry L. Martin* ....................................... xiii
1. The Beginning ............................................................... 1
2. The Nature of Revelation ............................................ 17
3. The Purpose of the Revelation ................................... 37
4. The Nature of the Divine Reality ............................... 51
5. The Big Picture ............................................................ 65
6. The Problem of Evil .................................................... 83
7. Nature of Human Beings .......................................... 105
8. World Religions ......................................................... 125
9. Eastern Religions ....................................................... 151
10. The Essential Project of the Divine ........................ 169
11. The Takeaway ........................................................... 195
12. Conclusion: How to Live ........................................ 221
*References* ...................................................................... 245
*Index* ............................................................................... 249
*Caladium Publishing* ..................................................... 257
*Theology Without Walls* ................................................ 259
*About the Authors* ......................................................... 261

*Acknowledgments*

Thanks are due to the invaluable work of creative director Scott Langdon, project manager Laura Buck, and Amanda Horgan for document preparation. It is to them that this book is dedicated.

*Foreword – By Jerry L. Martin*

This book owes its origins to an unplanned encounter. It took place in Boston, at an American Academy of Religion conference. I had attended a presentation on "radical evil" that had struck me as profound. The speaker was the philosopher Dr. Richard Oxenberg. I introduced myself afterwards and he said, "Oh, you're Jerry Martin." Selections from *God: An Autobiography, As Told to a Philosopher* had been posted on the internet in advance of publication. Dr. Oxenberg had been fascinated by what he read and immediately began to ask me a host of penetrating questions.

Subsequently, we scheduled long-distance conversations about the book. He suggested a series of topics that seemed to me of the greatest interest to serious seekers. Those discussions were turned into a podcast series featured on *God: An Autobiography as Told to a Philosopher - The Podcast* which can be found at godanautobiography.com.

*Two Philosophers Wrestle with God: A Dialogue* is the result.

# 1. The Beginning

**Dr. Jerry L. Martin** What every author most wants and needs is a really good reader, someone who reads their book carefully and thoughtfully. That is harder to come by than you would think. I use the word author advisedly since *God: An Autobiography, As Told to a Philosopher* reports what God told me verbatim from the notes I took as I prayed. God does most of the talking.

Dialogues are the classic form in which thinkers with different points of view converge on a common set of questions and concerns. It is a double blessing to find a really good reader who is also willing to engage in a serious discussion of the book.

I am blessed to have met Richard Oxenberg at a conference. It turned out that he had been reading the book and was eager to talk with me about it. What is remarkable about Richard Oxenberg is his preparation for reading such a book and his keenness in exploring and questioning it. Dr. Oxenberg is a professor of philosophy and world religions and has read the God book more carefully than anyone I know, including me. I find that he often will cite passages, things God had told me which, at the moment, I was forgetting. Thank you for initiating these dialogues, Richard.

**Dr. Richard Oxenberg** Good to see you, Jerry. I'm glad to be able to have this dialogue with you. Your experiences raise endless questions worth exploring. The title of your book is *God: An Autobiography,*

*As Told to a Philosopher*, so I'm going to assume that if God chose a philosopher to tell God's story to, God won't mind our raising some philosophical questions.

Why don't we begin, though, with your own story? Can you say a bit about how all this started for you?

**Jerry:** When God first spoke to me, I did not believe in God. I had been an agnostic my whole adult life and maybe back into childhood though it is hard to trace. I was a happy agnostic. Some people worry over whether there is a God or there is not a God. I had found a lot of wisdom in the philosophical tradition, so that was not a burning question for me. The question was not on my agenda at all. I had not even studied the philosophy of religion, much less any of the world's religions. Yet I did have a remarkable experience.

Having been divorced for a number of years, my future wife, Abigail, called me on the phone one day, and we became engaged in a project that led us to talk almost daily. In the course of those conversations, I fell in love with her—on the phone, sight unseen!

I managed to court her via Amtrak. She was in New York teaching at Brooklyn College. I was in Washington, D.C., running a higher education organization where she had called me for help.

The striking thing is that people often write about dramatic conversion experiences. For me, the conversion experience was falling in love. I did not even believe in love. I was looking for compatibility, like what dating services provide, listing your interests and hobbies, and the values that matter most.

But this was not like that. It was more like lightning lit up the world. It was as though I had lived in a black-and-white world, and the world suddenly had color. I lived in a two-dimensional world, and now it had depth. That was dramatic for me. My life went from a collection of purposes to having a *meaning*.

Love had totally changed my life, and yet I had done nothing to bring it about. It was like a miracle. It was certainly a dramatic intervention into my life and a blessing. A total blessing.

## THE BEGINNING

One day, I felt this overwhelming urge to fall to my knees and say a prayer. I reverted to the kind of religious training I had as a child. And I addressed a prayer of thanks to, I didn't know what word to use, the "Lord."

Though I did not know who the Lord was. The God of Israel? Jesus? Lord Krishna? A benign universe? I did not worry over that question because I knew this was an authentic feeling. And although I had no beliefs about a recipient of such a prayer, I did not see any reason I should not be expressing a genuine, overwhelming, authentic feeling. And so I did.

My act of praying did not change my belief system. I thought, "Well, that was just a momentary effusion," and went on about my business. About a month later, I had the same welling up, and this time when I offered a prayer of thanks, I added out of the blue, to the Lord in whom I did not believe, an offer to be of service. Once again, I did not make much of my heart-felt prayer. It was merely an emotional moment, and I just went on with my life.

At about that time, Abigail and I had a problem. Abigail was a tenured professor in New York. I was head of an organization in Washington, D.C., and we did not want a commuting marriage, even less an affair. We wanted to create a life together. How were we going to do that?

One day, sitting on a park bench on the Potomac, opposite the Lincoln Memorial, without forethought, I silently prayed again, this time for guidance. I was not thinking, "I'd better ask God what to do about this." It just welled up as a natural question because it looked unsolvable.

"Lord, how are we going to solve this?"

Immediately, there was a visual experience. In the old days, they would have called it a vision. It was like a hologram—a rising sparkling, multicolored fountain. I took it as positive assurance that things would work out. The life force is moving in the right direction, and things will work out.

But there was more. A voice spoke. I knew it was not me speaking. I turned to see if Abigail had heard it. She was sitting on a park bench beside me, writing in her journal. She kept writing, undisturbed.

So I asked, "Who is this?"

"**I am God.**"

I did not know much about religion, but I knew there were a lot of them and, hence, in a sense, many gods. I said, "The God of Israel?"

"**I am the God of all.**"

I did not at that moment ponder the implication. How does that answer the question? What does that mean exactly? I just thought, "Wow, I have just had an experience. God has just entered my life."

I had had a naturalistic worldview. Like new data from a scientific experiment, that view was hereby disconfirmed. My agnosticism went out the window.

**Richard:** Did you feel that right away upon hearing the voice for the first time? Did you question what this was, or did you immediately sense that this is God?

**Jerry:** Both. Inside the experience, it was undoubtedly God. The voice was too real, benign, and authoritative to really doubt. However, I am a philosopher. Doubting is what we do, right? We question everything. That got Socrates killed, running around, questioning, "Do you really know what you think you know?"

So, I could step outside the experience and say that the easiest thing in the world to be deluded about is a divine voice, like people in Times Square with placards that say, "the world's about to end." They think God is talking to them. So, of course, I had to doubt it.

I knew I could not just stay within the experience; I also had to look at the experience from the outside. I had to acknowledge the authority of the experience, even as I scrutinized it. I did have to go through that process of critical examination, especially since the voice continued to be available to me.

**Richard:** Abigail was sitting right next to you. Did you mention it to her?

**Jerry:** Only afterward. Looking at her, I was not surprised that she did not hear it. I thought it was a voice just for me, but I would not have been surprised if she had heard it because it came from outside. After the first time, there were further occasions when God spoke up, sometimes answering prayer, sometimes out of the blue, and sometimes it startled me.

**Richard:** And you never had an experience like this before?

**Jerry:** Not at all like this. Abigail also asked me that question at some point. I first said no, but then I remembered two experiences (recorded in the book) from my early life, but neither one had the drama of God speaking. They were not verbal.

**Richard:** They sounded more vague, experiences of moments of transcendence.

**Jerry:** Something familiar to many religious and non-religious people in moments where there is a kind of sacredness.

**Richard:** The voice of God has a distinctive sound as you express it: calmness, a sense of authority, and a sense of benignity.

**Jerry:** Completely benign. I tried to do whatever the voice told me to do because it had natural authority.

**Richard:** Was the experience of the fountain the only visual experience?

**Jerry:** The only thing that you would call a vision. I had an I/Thou relationship with a drop of water when I was in junior high. There was so little to the experience that at first I did not remember it, but it never went away because it was striking. It was as though that drop of water had a lot more to it than I could imagine and deserved a kind of reciprocity or respect.

**Richard:** It struck me in reading the book that there is a clear connection between your experience of falling in love with Abigail and your having this experience of God, as if the one was the condition for the other or created the possibility of the other.

**Jerry:** Love opened the door that previously had been closed. But it was not immediately obvious to me to believe in God as a consequence. It was not so much a change coming from my decision-making side as that being in love opened my soul. I had developed armor after being divorced for many years. I remember feeling that the armor needed to come off for Abigail and me—to let in the love.

**Richard:** The vision of the fountain almost seems like a graphic of how this feels—multicolored and rising.

**Jerry:** That was an empowering, soul-opening experience.

## THE BEGINNING

**Richard:** You do not go into your religious background very much in the book. When you had your experience, you say you were a "pious agnostic." Yet, throughout the book, it becomes apparent that you have knowledge of the Bible and a certain discomfort when you hear God say things contrary to the Bible.

To better understand where you came from and the differences between what God tells you in the book and what traditional religion tells us, maybe say a little about your religious background. Where did you grow up? Did your parents attend church? Did you attend church with them? How religious were they?

**Jerry:** The earliest church-going I can remember was when my family lived in Memphis, Tennessee, home base for the Martin family. We lived in the attic apartment of the house owned by my dad's parents, and my grandmother, the lady of the house, was Pentecostal.

My dad ran his own little company selling pens and calendars to businesses, and he was a very ethical businessman. So I learned a lot from watching him and the occasional preachments. My earliest memories of my dad were of him going to Memphis State University on a G.I. Bill, getting degrees, and preparing to go on in life. My mother was working at Sears.

There was not much religiosity in the home of those two parents. Later in life, at Thanksgiving, I asked my dad if he wanted to say Grace, and he said, "No, my prayers wouldn't pass the ceiling."

My mother was a very simple Baptist, very literal and puzzled by it all. She was also very smart and canny. At the end of her life, she was afraid she would not go to heaven, and I had to reassure her. She said, "How do you know?" She was probing and hard to answer.

**Richard:** Were they still alive when you first began to have these experiences?

**Jerry:** Yes. Both had long lives. My mother was a high school senior when my dad met her. He went for her and dropped by the school every day. He was 19 but already working the way people did back then in the Texas panhandle. My mother had grown up in a little Baptist Church, in a tiny town of a thousand people, and did not finish high school, but she was a very, very clever, shrewd woman.

Because of my grandmother's presence, we went to the Pentecostal church in Memphis. Frankly, I found it scary. They would speak in tongues and go off in rants. Even in Sunday school, where you are supposed to be looking at nice stories about Jesus, the teacher would carry on with tears flowing down her cheeks. I was disturbed: What's going on?

My parents later moved to California. My dad was stationed in San Diego, and they liked the climate, so they left Memphis and moved to San Diego. While we were in California, Oral Roberts came to town. He was a fantastic evangelist and gave a very moving, tremendous sermon. I can remember it still, the part where Judas Iscariot commits suicide. Oral Roberts is saying, "Don't do it! Don't do it, Judas," while, at the same time, making a noose out of the chord of his microphone and looping it around his head.

The Baptists taught that if you die before the age of reason, about 12 years old, you automatically go to heaven. So, I had in my mind, "I am at the age of reason now. I'd better cover my bets." So I went forward. It was almost like Pascal's Wager, placing bets on the best outcomes.

They sent me to a side tent with a very nice woman to pray over me. I remember hoping I would feel transformed or saved. It was very cold, with a chill in the air. I was down on my knees on the damp ground, teeth chattering. I thought and hoped this was a spiritual experience, but, no, I was just uncomfortable. I thanked the nice woman, and I filled out her card. Those were the kinds of experiences I had.

The problem is that, if you are in a Baptist environment and have the mentality of a philosopher, you are full of questions and you are a bit of a rationalist, so you need an answer for everything. The Baptists I was around did not have answers for anything, or the answers were extraordinarily shallow, hardly counting as answers at all. I do not have a skeptical temperament, exactly, but I wondered about things. There were inconsistencies between what they said and how they lived.

As a child, I could never figure out why everybody cried so much when a child died. The child had escaped hell, the chief hazard of life, going automatically to heaven. Why was somebody talking so much about Sunday clothing? I thought it was supposed to be the state of your soul that mattered. Not, "Did you wash behind your ears," and "isn't that a nice dress?"

In spite of the theology being so flimsy, I credit that religious background and continue to value the sense that the state of your soul is the most important thing in life. This was what the wisest of the philosophers had taught. I did not need to look back to religion. You can live a noble life if you live it according to the wisdom of Plato and Aristotle.

**Richard:** As a child, did you have an image of what God was like in your mind?

**Jerry:** I did not have much of an image. The church had images, and I found them often off-putting, and puzzling.

**Richard:** Off-putting because they were frightening?

**Jerry:** Frankly, the images of Jesus on the cross and a little loincloth hanging looked sensual. He has this lithe body, is completely toned, and is quite skimpy on clothing. That seemed odd. The focus in that church is so much on Jesus that one does not even think that much about God, the Father, and how God the Father might look.

I did not wonder about what kind of being God was. The Baptists take the stories in a full-hearted way, while more sophisticated theologians, and maybe traditions with a bigger intellectual side, such as the Catholics and the Calvinists, have a whole apparatus for that.

I did not have a visual image of God. It is more like just a voice from nowhere. In the Old Testament, the voice speaks out, because you do not see God. But, no, I was not afraid of the Old Testament God.

**Richard:** You speak of your mother fearing that she wasn't going to go to heaven.

**Jerry:** The church we attended in California was a little Baptist church. I rather liked the minister. He was a scholarly fellow. He would talk of the Greek New Testament and explicate the meaning of this word and that word. Many congregants criticized him because he did not do the "hell and brimstone" pitch and bring the souls to Christ.

**Richard:** But you didn't walk around worrying that a wrathful God might condemn you?

**Jerry:** No, no. Many people do that, I know many people with a religious upbringing go around feeling guilty all the time, under the eye of the divine inquisitor. I felt guilty, but the same guilt I felt when I was an agnostic, you know, just about my personal failings.

**Richard:** Can you remember a distinctive moment when you finally decided that you did not believe in God anymore?

**Jerry:** For my high school friends, this was a big question. Is there a God? One woman was a Christian Scientist, educated more than we were. She talked about Spinoza, Berkeley, and some philosophers that fed into the Christian science way of thinking. God was a question for us. During freshman year in college, I decided, given the back and forth of various arguments, that there was no way to settle this question. I decided: I will just postulate, in my young rationalist mode, that there is a God, and I will just live with that.

But "God" was just a word, an empty word. None of us seemed to worry over that; we were not that sophisticated. I did not even have a definition of an infinite being or something like that. There were all these different religions, theologies, conceptions, but all I had was just an empty word.

Most people would immediately build their own tradition right into the word, "God." They would build into the word the particular idea of God they learned about in their community.

But I was too much of a rationalist to make that move. So all I had was an empty postulate. All the classic arguments for the existence of God were shot down in philosophy class. It is really hard to prove God with just an argument. You can prove maybe some kind of being that sounds rather abstract. Meanwhile, I found that other things I was learning in philosophy were adequate for living a life of high purpose.

One of my teachers was the estimable Philip Wheelwright, author of *The Burning Fountain*, who was both richly educated and wise. He called himself a pious agnostic. Since then, I have thought of him as a humanist with a very high ceiling. Some humanists have very low ceilings. They are really reductionists of some kind, for whom there is only matter. Wheelwright was not like that at all. He thought being a human was an amazing thing, that the world was an amazing place with depth and meaning. One of his cardinal rules was, "Never say 'nothing but,' never say 'this is all.'"

So it was an open-ended ceiling, though for him, never filled in by a belief in something higher; it was T.S. Eliot and Dante. Wheelwright quotes a Finnish myth in one of his books, the lesson of which is "to sing the full song."

Being open is very natural to me. I tend to believe in experience. In spite of the logical turn of mind I have described, I am actually not much of a rationalist. I have never thought, "If I cannot make logical sense of it, then it is not so. It has no meaning and cannot be true." If you do that, you close off your experience.

Some types of psychology treat love that way. It is really just projection, and it is just biochemistry. Somebody attributed my falling in love with Abigail to pheromones. People take love, honor, duty, and everything, and they reduce it all to biochemistry. Wheelwright said, "No, accept the rich view of human experience and take it all in."

**Richard:** So, you came to think of yourself as an agnostic. Of course, agnosticism is not atheism.

**Jerry:** No. That is why I was never an atheist. That never appealed to me. It seemed to imply that you have done a complete inventory of everything in the universe and God is not there. How could you know that?

**Richard:** I think the atheist begins by rejecting a particular conception of God, say the God of Western religion, or the God of the Bible. And then, if you can't fill it in with anything else, at that point you call yourself an atheist.

**Jerry:** Yes. They are rejecting a very specific conception of God. They think atheism is the only alternative to this simplistic or scary conception they reject.

**Richard:** How has your experience of yourself and the world changed through this new encounter with God?

**Jerry:** In my worldview, it has made me much more open to what you might call bizarre experiences. If God can talk to me, then anything is possible. I am now much more open and inclined to credit coincidences as divine guidance. If I have trouble getting to an appointment because the trains are not running, my first question now is, "Is this a message for me?" I do not assume that it is. It is very hard to connect these dots, after all, but I do view the world as having a lot more meaning than before.

Before, the world had a kind of syntax with no semantics. It was just a pile of things. Also, my experience has made me more tolerant of small interferences. For example, I am nicer in traffic now. I do not have to be the first one there. Let them go first.

**Richard:** What is it about experiencing the presence of God that makes someone nicer in traffic?

**Jerry:** It is a surrender to the Divine. My own will is not the main thing anymore, whereas my will was everything before. My wife certainly notices the difference. The change is from my will being number one to, at tops, number two in the world, and perhaps as a good husband, number three.

**Richard:** I suppose to surrender authentically, one has to feel in touch with that to which one *can* surrender. It might not be so easy to surrender.

**Jerry:** That is absolutely true. It always seems to be one of those arguments for the existence of God they shoot down. That is the argument from religious experience, based on an experience of the Divine, either directly in my dramatic way or, like Buber, through an I/thou encounter with nature, which he said extends then to the eternal thou, or through what taking the Eucharist might do for a Catholic. If you have that moment where you sense there is a divine element in the universe, and you realize its extraordinary specialness (after all, it is not simply another fact about the universe), it becomes very natural to want to be in harmony with that divine element.

**Richard:** I would think it also helps you to feel not so alone.

**Jerry:** One of the huge differences in religiosity is that theists are never alone. You are never alone. The other day, I was talking to Abigail about some novelist who writes, "Everybody dies alone." I do not think that way. If I were dying and Abigail was by my side, I am not dying alone. And God is present. You are aware that God is present at every moment if you have the kind of experience I have had. This is a huge life change.

**Richard:** That is a palpable experience for you now, something you always have with you.

**Jerry:** Yes. I get distracted, but if I pause, meditate, and pray, I feel God inside me. Like many religious people, I have that kind of experience with God, Jesus, and Krishna, inside and outside, watching over me. It gives, as Augustine discovered, your whole life a kind of drama because it is not just one thing after another anymore. It is the unfolding of something. For God, that must have ultimate meaning. You have got to create as meaningful a life as you possibly can—because you have the primo audience of the world.

**Richard:** Your experience of God is very direct, real, and concrete; this is not some abstract idea of God that you arrived at through reflection. You've had a direct encounter with God. The question that occurs to me is: Why doesn't everyone have such an encounter? What prevents it? Presumably, it is not God withholding Godself, so what would it be?

**Jerry:** It is a very fundamental question. Why is it that some people have these experiences while others do not? I have had correspondence with people who are angry, praying and praying, earnestly asking to speak to God. They ask, sometimes angrily, why God spoke to this guy who was not even a believer instead of them. Let us hold the question for next time because it requires a multi-part answer. That is a burning question.

**Richard:** It is a burning question.

## THE BEGINNING

**Jerry:** For the skeptic, it is a question because you think if there is a God and that God can speak, then surely God would be speaking to everyone. If God is not, then that casts doubt on experiences of divine encounter.

**Richard:** Yes. This is certainly a fundamental question for the philosophy of religion and spirituality: Why is God so difficult to experience?

**Jerry:** We should look at whether there is anything a person can do to bring about a closer connection to God and discover what God wants of them.

**Richard:** This is a question that will come up throughout our discussions- specifically with respect to your revelatory experiences. How and why did they come to you, and how might your experience of revelation compare with other reports of revelation?

**Jerry:** And answer: Why a new revelation now?

**Richard:** These are some of the questions we'll explore in our next session. Thank you, Jerry.

# 2. The Nature of Revelation

**Dr. Jerry L. Martin** As any pursuer of the truth knows, what you most need to help you along the way is good questions, and so we continue to deal with the kinds of questions that a rather rich book like *God: An Autobiography* raises.

**Dr. Richard Oxenberg** I thought today we would focus on questions concerning the nature of revelation. If I were to run into Isaiah, Mohammed, or anyone else who professed to have had a direct revelation from God, I'd have a few questions to ask about the nature of their experience. How did it occur? What was it like? What kind of authority are we to grant it? Do we have to accept it at face value, or is there any 'wiggle room' that we have in interpreting it?

For instance, if Mohammed says, "I heard God tell me this," do we have to accept that every word he heard is directly of God? Are we faced with the choice of either accepting the divine status of everything he reports or rejecting everything? Or might there be a middle ground? And if there is a middle ground, what might there be about the nature of revelation that would *allow for* that middle ground?

**Jerry:** Good questions. Is it appropriate to make use of a revelation reasonably and intelligently? Must we accept, in Mohammed's report, every word and every comma as the word of God or is the only alternative to reject such reports as though God is not going to talk to Isaiah, or Mohammed, or anybody.

**Richard:** One reason I ask this question has to do with my own way of approaching texts like the Bible. I believe there is a sense in which the Bible is inspired by higher truth, but at the same time, I am unable to believe that every word we read in the Bible is a word chosen by God—or that it is necessary to follow the Bible in a literalistic, absolutistic, manner. In fact, I find that a literal approach to the Bible can actually get in the way of understanding its deeper message. So this leads to questions about how exactly revelation works.

Let me start, then, by asking you to tell us something about your own revelatory experiences. How exactly did you experience the voice of God? Did it always come to you in the same way, or were there times when it was fainter and others when it was more pronounced? In the book, you put your own words in quotation marks and God's words in boldface.

**Jerry:** The text identifies the voice of God with boldface.

**Richard:** Were you writing these words down as you were speaking with God? Taking dictation?

**Jerry:** I was taking dictation.

**Richard:** From memory? Or were you sitting there with a pad and pen and writing it down as you heard it? How exactly did that work?

**Jerry:** I am reporting it as I remember it in the first couple of chapters of the book. At a certain point, as the prayers progressed, I found I could pray and get answers to questions that I had both as a spiritual seeker and a philosopher. At that point, I saw I needed to start taking notes. For me, I find that is the best way to pray. I sit down with a pad and write out my questions. Sometimes the answer

## THE NATURE OF REVELATION

starts coming before I get the whole question written, and then I am taking dictation. I have shortened parts to avoid repetition, because it is very important to keep distinct what God told Jerry from what Jerry thinks, thought about it, or extrapolated from it.

**Richard:** When you say you are taking dictation, do you hear the words sounding in your mind?

**Jerry:** Sometimes I hear the words first but often I do not know the word I am writing before writing it. The words come out of me through my writing them.

**Richard:** Did you ever find yourself saying to God, "Hey, slow down?"

**Jerry:** I had a terrible time keeping up. Some of my notes are just scrawls. I save them all for future reference. It came so fast, and it was very hard to keep up. As I said, sometimes, before I get the question formulated, the answer is coming, and I have to manage that.

I treated the God quotes with punctilious care. How would I be in a position to edit them? I am just Jerry Martin. How would I be able to say a part was wrong, better, or worse? Some answers contradict an earlier answer. I have left both in because maybe they are both true if you understand them a certain way or perhaps the later version supersedes an earlier one. I am getting more tuned in and certainly learning as I go along. God says to read, "So I have something to work with." I need some equipment in my head because it is my head that God is using.

**Richard:** In the book, now and then, you include parentheses in the middle of God's statement to make what God said a little clearer to the reader.

**Jerry:** I put in a little "or" because often it came to me as phrases right after another, and that is hard for the reader. This happens in conversation. The two of you understand what you are talking about, and the sense of it, so I am just putting that in to help the reader. It shows my scrupulousness with regard to the actual words because I am adding those interpretive elements with the parentheses around them.

**Richard:** Your experience was very much that of someone engaged in a conversation with another person who is somehow conversing with you inside your own mind. It wasn't just inspiration.

**Jerry:** Yes, exactly. It is not an inspiration in a poetic sense. Occasionally, I am wondering, "Is this still God talking?" It is natural in conversation where you almost start completing each other's sentences- a kind of extrapolating thought. I am then usually told by God, "No, that was all from Me," though at that point it felt more like thinking than it did like listening.

**Richard:** Another question I have is the extent to which you may have been, in some manner, contributing to the revelation yourself. It often seems to me that God's style of speaking in the book is very much like your own style of speaking. In other words, I do not get a sense that this is a distinctively 'divine' style of speaking. I imagine that if I were to meet the spirit of Shakespeare, he would speak like Shakespeare, not like me. But in the book God speaks very much like you. In one of the passages in the book you actually bring this up and God says to you, "Well, that is just the way that revelation works."

**Jerry:** I am always questioning this even as, at the same time, I am completely accepting it. I am believing the divine voice, acting on it, giving up a career and working to follow this voice. If God is going to speak to me, why does it sound just like me? It is my conversational style. Of course, the content is not at all what I previously believed. Some readers have said "No, it does not really sound like Jerry."

**Richard:** Well, it does and it doesn't. The content often came to you as a surprise.

**Jerry:** Yes, and the language is sometimes corrected. Why does God speak, unlike Shakespeare come to life again, in our way? Because we are the instruments. At one point there was a moment when I felt pride because I am hearing from God! That makes me rather special. Of course, the first thing that happened was the line went dead. I had been in lively relation to God and that moment of ego just cut it off. I was then told,

> **"You are no more special than the paint Leonardo happened to use in the Mona Lisa."**

If you are just paint, it is good to make it into the Mona Lisa. On the other hand, paint is just paint. It illustrates that I am God's palette in this set of revelations. Mohammed had a very different palette. Isaiah, and Jeremiah, another palette.

**Richard:** A critically important point, it seems to me. Another way of putting it might be: God is the sculptor and you are the clay.

**Jerry:** Yes. Or the marble, perhaps.

**Richard:** Or we might think of God's situation as like an artist who wants to present an image of a three-dimensional object, but only has a two-dimensional page to present it on.

**Jerry:** We start with equipment as it is. It may be wrenched and bended and then adapted. Artists do that with their materials. An artist thinks of a new way to portray something with an instrument, a new way to fashion it. God is changing the instrumentality, changing, opening my mind, heart, and soul in new ways, so that more can come in and so that God can do more with this particular instrumentality. That seems to be the nature of revelation.

That is how God comes to people in their own situation, in their own terms, maybe even in response to their own needs. Some of the prophets are very much people addressing particular historical situations. There is a tendency, I think, to overly relativize this sort of thing. You start saying, "Well, it's bounded in this way, bounded by that way, and it sounds like just a perspective." If you think of art, why are we glad that there is a Rembrandt and a Van Gogh and a Picasso? Each one is limited in their own way, but they show you the world in different ways. God is using Jerry Martin to show the world in the way that God feels is needed for Jerry Martin or, maybe even more, for our particular historical time.

**Richard:** Clearly, the revelation you receive is for more than just you.

**Jerry:** It is not really personal or just for Jerry. I pray, "Why are we doing this?" The answer is in terms of the state of religion today.

**Richard:** Might we say that the nature of the human relation to God is such that we can only experience God as qualified by our own limitations? We can only experience God in the way that God can be experienced by a human being. Or we might go even further and say: I can only experience God in the way that God can be experienced by Richard Oxenberg, and you can only experience God in the way God can be experienced by Jerry Martin. Of course, this doesn't mean that the revelation cannot have relevance for other people as well.

Nevertheless, when God speaks through you, what we hear is God filtered through Jerry Martin. When we hear God speaking through Mohammed, we are hearing God filtered through Mohammed. And

## THE NATURE OF REVELATION

we can say the same thing about Isaiah or any other prophet. There is a filtering process that is integral to the very nature of revelation, such that we never get God in an unadulterated form.

**Jerry:** The problem if you talk that way is it starts sounding as though we never get God at all. I remember G. E. Moore, the British philosopher, in his remarkable carefulness, when he is visiting a zoo, and someone says, "That is a huge elephant." "Well, from this side at least," says Moore. There is something odd about that statement. What does that mean? It looks huge to us. It is how a huge elephant is showing itself and looks under these circumstances.

God is showing God's self through these various lenses. It is as if I have looked at the moon through a telescope. Your vision is filtered by the telescope, its lens and so forth. However, it is not exactly right to call this a limitation. The telescope is empowering your perception to see the moon and so, you are seeing more. You are seeing the craters, which you could not see before. I see these as empowerments. There is a lot to God and God can show many things about Godself by using the vocabulary and historical circumstances of Jerry Martin, as God did of Isaiah. But you are right, the telescope is there.

**Richard:** I ask this because I am wondering about the question of inerrancy. In the book we have the boldface text, which are the words of God as you heard them and diligently recorded them. Could they still be in error? Let us suppose that you recorded the words of God just as you heard them, and entered them into the book just as you recorded them—could there still be error? Could what we read in the boldface text still misrepresent what is true of God? In biblical theology, there are doctrines of infallibility and doctrines of inerrancy. What is the relationship of the revelation that we read in your book with respect to such doctrines? Are the boldface words infallible or inerrant?

**Jerry:** There still could be errors. There are kinds of inerrancy but, in fact, I am told pointedly that I am a fallible receptor. It depends on where you are trying to locate the error. God makes grammatical mistakes in these transcripts; I do not correct them; I leave them there. I do not know if there are factual mistakes. There are times where God used a word that did not quite seem the right word. God was telling me to read William of Ockham very early on. I thought God meant Anselm. Why would I want to read Ockham?
And I said, "Do you mean Anselm?"

"**No. No. William of Ockham.**"

So there is that wiggle room, not in a way much different from going to interview Winston Churchill about what happened during the war. The interviewer is writing notes. The interviewer could make a mistake, could misunderstand the words, could misunderstand the context. Churchill himself, though he was there, might have mistakes of memory or expression.

**Richard:** But if the interviewer wrote down the words of Winston Churchill and wrote them down faithfully, then those words would be unmistakably, inerrantly, Winston Churchill's words. If one assumes that the words are coming from God, and that we have them accurately, then they must, at the very least, be a reflection of how God understands reality to be. These are the words that God chose to use, and you recorded them just as you heard them. So, then, in what sense could you be a fallible receptor?

**Jerry:** If you think about the early prayers, where I knew nothing, God had very little to work with because I had never been interested in religion, and had not studied religion, even the religion I was raised in. I really just had the childhood pictures that were all I knew of Christianity. And, so, a lot of my early questions were rather crude formulations. God answers those, much the way a professor in a

## THE NATURE OF REVELATION

class will answer freshmen, saying "yes that is correct," but meaning really, that is close enough. In teaching, you cannot go into every nuance and complication. You are trying to get some basic point across. God is saying, basically, to me as a neophyte, "Jerry, you are on the right track. Yes, that will do."

Later, I learned a great deal more. One instructive passage, on page 271, is in the context of earlier prayers that are somewhat discounted, I get the sense that I should focus on who I am talking to:

> "Lord, I have the sense that I should focus on Jesus' message of love—and let it into my own heart. I need to set aside my uneasy feelings with 'washed in the blood' and other echoes of my childhood. Is that right, Lord?"
>
> **"Both points are correct. Also, listen to Jesus' human voice. At this point, also bracket our earlier prayers, which were contaminated in various ways."**

Apparently, earlier prayers, perhaps because I didn't yet know what questions to ask or how to understand the answers, were less authoritative and should be understood in the context of later prayers. Then Jesus spoke to me:

> **"Don't be so worried about all this. Don't be too wedded to the scripture. This is not exegesis that we're doing. You know what I am about, which is the healing power of love."**

**Richard:** I am asking these questions from a theoretical point of view, but also because, at a much more personal level, there are passages in the book I find questionable. Not in the sense that I do not understand them, but that I find them hard to believe. I can give you my various reasons for this, but there are passages that just don't ring true to me, ring holy to me, or seem like what God would say.

In my experience of reading the book, I'll be finding it absolutely fascinating, and then I will run into rough patches where it just does not seem right, and this leads to the dilemma I spoke about earlier: Do I have to either totally accept or totally reject the words in boldface, or is there a middle ground where I can say to myself that, though Jerry is accurately recording what he heard, the nature of revelation is such that it can get contaminated, so that the words professed to be of God might not truly be of God?

**Jerry:** All scriptures have those characteristics. The Old Testament has horrible moments like when they are told to kill every man, woman, child, and animal of the Amalekites. How could that be a Godly thing to instruct people to do? The questions of literalists come up here, but there is a sort of double process of reception. I am the instrument of God's revelation. You, Richard, you are the instrument in reading this version of this revelation from God. The way to read *God: An Autobiography* is accepting that there is yet another revelation, and that is the revelation to Richard (or to the reader).

I advise readers to find out what parts of the book speak to them, because that is the part that God is trying to get through to that reader. I do not emphasize the fact that everybody is limited but emphasize empowerment. Richard brings different things than another reader, and so, Richard is able to see things there and appropriate them or make use of them in ways that the next person over might miss.

One person, a very good reader who is much more of a practical person, is looking at how to do good in the world. Parts of the book she was drawing insight from, that are being revealed to her, were very much more relevant and put into the terms of her life. That is being revealed to her through the book.

## THE NATURE OF REVELATION

The Hebrew Bible was like this. Genesis 1 and Genesis 3 give accounts of Adam and Eve that read quite differently. Those apparent inconsistencies occur repeatedly. Someone had to put all these disparate elements received from oral tradition together, and that is the one they call the "Great Redactor." A redactor is like an editor who decides which texts go into the final version and in what order.

The Great Redactor is a somewhat mysterious character. We have a good guess about who it was, but it is perfectly possible that God is also leading the Great Redactor. God may be leading the Great Redactor to include contradictory elements. In the New Testament, the chronologies of Jesus vary from one gospel to another. They kept all four gospels in, and the differences may not even matter.

**Richard:** That makes a lot of sense as a practical approach to reading any kind of revelatory scripture. We can ask: What resonates with me? What makes sense to me? I guess the question for me, though, as a philosopher, as someone who is trying to understand the nature of revelation, is: What justifies me in saying that a particular passage, professed to contain the words of God, is not true?

Let me tell you the way I have come to think of it, and you can tell me whether this sounds right to you or not. There is a divide, of course, between you and God. God is the issuer of revelation, and you are the receiver. One question we can ask is: Where exactly does the divide fall? One way to make sense of the fallibility of revelation is to say that the divide falls *prior* to the formation of words, prior to the production of the actual words that are being recorded in boldface, such that the words themselves are being formed by you, your mind, not by God.

In other words, though God is truly inspiring your mind to come up with these words, the ideas that God is trying to convey exist in a supra-linguistic form. In order to turn them into language, God needs, so to speak, a language machine, and the recipient of revelation is that language machine. God does not have a language or a linguistic style of God's own. God is using the language machine that comes from your mind, your brain. That's why the style sounds like you. Somehow, the supra-linguistic idea issued by God is stimulating your language machine, perhaps at an unconscious level, to come up with words that may or may not be perfect reflections of the supra-linguistic idea itself.

To give you a sense of what I'm saying, God talks about feeling lonely right at the beginning of creation. Then God has this interesting moment where God says, "What I mean by loneliness may not be what you mean by loneliness."

In other words, you can only understand what loneliness means in terms of how it feels for a human being to be lonely, and that is going to be your best approximation to what God is talking about. But maybe what God is actually talking about goes way beyond anything that can be expressed in human language.

This is how I would make sense of the fallibility of revelation. God is presenting to your mind a supra-linguistic truth that is getting processed into the actual language we read in the book by your own cognitive and linguistic faculties, which may not always be able to fully express, or even understand, the supra-linguistic idea. This would allow me to account for the fact that there are boldface passages in the book that seem to me not quite right.

**Jerry:** I have nothing against using whatever conceptual apparatus helps, but it all feels completely unnatural to me. I am like the paint that Leonardo used. I am God's paint. At one point, God used the image of the quill. I am the quill. That reflects my experience more than the instrumentality of an English speaking person available to God and God just uses that person. To me, it seemed more like the way Europeans speak English. It is marvelous. If a European comes to the United States and starts speaking English, he or she is not having a supra language that he or she is using, entering it into English. Why can't God do that? That fits the experience, and it seems to fit the analogies offered.

## THE NATURE OF REVELATION

**Richard:** But I think if that were the case there wouldn't be the discrepancies and fallibilities we see within and between revealed texts. For instance, according to the book, Zoroaster was the recipient of a true revelation from God, but he somehow managed to interpret it as there being two Gods—one good and one evil. Pagans received true revelations presumably, but somehow managed to turn this into a belief in a multitude of nature gods. So is God just being coy with all these people? Is God thinking, "I will tell these people one thing and tell these other people something else and maybe thousands of years from now, they will piece it all together"?

It seems that we either have to envision God as kind of crafty in this way, or we have to say that the very nature of revelation is such that it is imperfect and incomplete and subject to distortion and error.

**Jerry:** These points you are raising now are answered in the book. Why there is a diversity of revelations, and why they are different, are questions answered in the book. It is not because God wanted to be tricky or merely communicated what this or that group of people had the capacity to hear and to receive. The different sides of God that emerge through history are mainly different aspects of God. The divine reality has multiple aspects recorded in multiple scriptures. That does not mean every line of every scripture is right. Zoroaster is a true revelation that shows something about the divine reality.

Subsequently, I read scholar Jon Levenson's book on the Hebrew Bible. Those same themes that are in Zoroaster are in the Old Testament, but in a different form. In a way, the Old Testament is an answer to Zoroaster because it develops beyond Zoroaster. This shows the developmental nature of God and of our relation to God. Part of the reason for the diversity is God's very complexity, which would be overwhelming for a single culture. Why could God not have given the people of Israel the task of the covenant and at the same time have them doing Hindu meditative practices and saying Ohm, or vice versa? That would have been overwhelming.

There is a specialization that fits the culture and fits the side of God that is becoming manifest through interacting with that culture. Because God is always emerging. I do not find the diversity of religions to be itself a problem for revelation. It occurs historically as God manifested in different ways to different people, and different cultures, according to their historical moments, and their capacity.

**Richard:** So, given this, we can't really attribute perfect or infallible truth to any particular revelation.

**Jerry:** It is like the Indian parable, "The Blind Men and the Elephant." In the story, blind men touch distinct parts of an elephant, and each forms a limited perspective on what an elephant is like based on the part they touched. Each man had the rash assumption that their piece was the whole elephant. It is natural to have only the legs and think the elephant is entirely like the leg. Someone else has the tail, and they think the elephant must be entirely like this tail- like a snake. It is not untrue in any way. But it did not occur to anybody to put these together.

One often gives different students different kinds of instructions. A clinical therapist will not do the same thing with one patient as with another because the cases are different. There is much of life where the fact that you are doing things differently from one case to another does not mean there is some fakery, falsehood, lying, or deception going on.

**Richard:** We may have a bit of a gap in our way of thinking about this. Let us consider the Bible for a moment. In the Old Testament, we have quite a few specific injunctions concerning how people should live and what laws they should follow. There are people who maintain that those laws were revealed by God and never revoked. Therefore, we have an obligation to live in accordance with those specific laws today.

So, what are we to say about this? Were these laws truly spoken by God or not? The Bible presents them as spoken by God. If we could go back to the original person who wrote these biblical passages, which declare that God said such-and-such, would he say, "Oh, I didn't really mean that to be taken literally. It was just an idea of what *I* thought people should do and I thought God would approve so I put it in God's mouth"? Or did the people who wrote these passages have experiences similar to yours? Were they also writing down what they somehow heard God say?

If we understand them to have written down what they heard God say, then what must our approach to these words be now? Must we accord them divine authority, or is it possible that—though the people who wrote them did have something analogous to your experience—what comes out of such an experience is not a perfect reflection of divine truth but rather an imperfect reflection?

If the latter, then this allows me to say, "That which speaks to me, that which inspires me, that which seems right and true and good to me, I can embrace as reflective of God. That which does not, I have an obligation to reject until such time as it does seem right and true and good to me." Looking at revelation as fallible in this way allows me to take this approach.

**Jerry:** There are dangers in either approach. If you take everything too wholly and literally as if it were the one and only and whole truth, then there are dangers of dogmatism. Things that were part of the life of people with whom God is interacting at a certain time are built into all eternity.

On the other hand, there is a danger in sifting through and picking and choosing. At one point God uses the expression, "The arrogance of human reason." We start thinking of the categorical imperative or the principle of utility or some later philosophical, rational structure. Then we go back and pick and choose the scripture that fits. The problem with that is not only that one might miss some truths, but it is a question of the openness of the soul. There is a big emphasis in the book on obedience and obedience is described as transforming. It is a kind of yielding of the soul. A major theme in various religious literatures and different traditions is the importance of yielding. Part of the arrogance of human reason is connected with ego, where we say, in effect, "I am going to use my reason as the supreme judge." That is the risk at that end.

**Richard:** I've always had a little trouble with the phrase, "the arrogance of human reason." Following reason is not necessarily arrogant. I suppose arrogance would come in if someone were to say: Only what I can conclude through my own reason can possibly be true, and whatever I can't conclude through my reason cannot possibly be true. The arrogance of human reason in this sense is taken care of by what I've come to think of as "Socratic humility."

Socrates was famous for saying, "I know that I don't know." But this doesn't mean that he didn't respect reason. Rather, he followed reason as far as it would take him and then said, "this is what I must conclude, given what my reason tells me, and I cannot conclude anything but this. Still, I am open to the possibility that I may be mistaken."

We might speak of Socrates' approach as, "the humility of human reason." But I don't think we want to abandon reason. If we abandon reason, what are we going to rely on for discerning the truth?

**Jerry:** We are not talking about abandoning reason. Let me approach this another way. When I was growing up, philosophy students were told to follow the principle of charity. If you read a philosopher and it does not seem to add up, you need to read it again to discover the sense it does make.

A. J. Ayer said that, when he read Plato, all he found were a bunch of bad arguments. If he had applied the principle of charity, he would have said, "Well, if they strike you as bad arguments, maybe you are not reading it right." You do not know. Maybe they are bad arguments, but don't rush to judgment: Go back and read it again.

The merit of the principle of charity as a heuristic, truth-seeking device is that it enables you to approach *God: An Autobiography* or the book of Genesis or Exodus, trying to learn from it. Let it teach me. You have to be careful not to hold its feet to the fire too much, prematurely, so that you are not able to be told more.

There is a medieval practice that I recommend from *God: An Autobiography* called *lectio divina*. It is often called "praying through the Bible." You do not just read; you pray and see what comes to you. You let the text speak to you, or let God speak to you through that text. That is a way to pull out the nuggets of truth that might not at first look like nuggets of truth.

**Richard:** I entirely agree with what you're saying here—it sounds a bit like what I have come to call a "dialectical" reading of scripture, where you enter into a dialogue with the reading. You question it and then look to it to find an answer to your question. And I would say that the idea of charitable reading is related to the idea of charitable interpretation. In other words, you try to find an interpretation that will make some sense of what you are reading. But, of course, it has to be a plausible interpretation. You have to be able to honestly say to yourself, "I am not twisting the words to make them say something they manifestly do not say."

One of the things that allows me to be charitable toward the Bible is to say to myself that I am not under any obligation to accept everything in it as the definitive word of God. Rather, I enter into a dialogue with the Bible, a dialectic with the Bible. And then I employ discernment in deciding what to accept and what not to accept. If I think there is something offensive about the idea that God has ordered the slaughter of all the Amalekites, for instance, I have to ask myself: Which should I give more credence to, the text or my moral sensibilities? Which should I follow? And my answer is my moral sensibilities.

**Jerry:** Or are there other options?

**Richard:** But maybe there are no other options. Maybe any other option would involve my reading in bad faith and attributing to the text what is not really there, or making myself an apologist for a text that is morally abhorrent. I prefer to say it is wrong. Somebody recorded it wrong. Somebody heard it wrong. Somebody perceived it wrong. Human beings are fallible receptors, as God says in your book.

**Jerry:** God uses that expression in *God: An Autobiography*. It is different when it is your own experience, of course.

**Richard:** Yes. This discussion also bears upon places in the book where God does not tell you something in particular but tells you to try to enter into God's experience. It is as if you enter into an empathic relationship with something that is coming to you from God, but—I would say anyway—your ability to have that empathic relationship is limited by what you can experience and understand within yourself. So, in understanding these passages we need to be open to the possibility that your experience of God may not be a perfect reflection of what God is. Of course, this may be a lot easier for me to say coming at it from some distance, than for you to say, having had this experience in such a profound way.

**Jerry:** My main job is to accurately report the experience, the words, and the dialogue, and where there are experiences, I am drawn into, guided into, to report those as they came to me. The reasons for this particular set of revelations in *God: An Autobiography* was for people to understand what it is like to be God. Most of our theology does not even think of what it is like to be God. I have Socratic humility and the sense that I am always arguing with God through the course of the book. God answers sometimes satisfactorily, to my mind, sometimes not. I just go on, or maybe come back to the same issue. One of the problems is that we see God only from the outside and not from what it is like to be God. The "outside" view makes God a distant kind of object, and that blocks the relationship, as it would with any person if you saw them only as, say, a public figure.

I saw this phenomenon in my years in Washington, D.C. If you see someone only as a public persona, then you are not relating to them at all. That is the outer crust of a real person. God wants us to relate in this deeper way where we empathize with God, and God empathizes with us. Empathizing does not mean to conjure up feeling. Empathy is a mode of perception and of understanding.

**Richard:** Perhaps what we can get out of this whole discussion so far is that, when we encounter any claim to revelation, we ought to read it, to the extent that we are going to take it seriously at all, with everything we've got.

**Jerry:** Sure, with heart, mind, and soul.

**Richard:** With our concerns, with our reason, with our knowledge. In doing so, we enter into a dialectic with it. And where truth seems to bubble up from that dialectic, we can hold onto that truth, a truth that has come to us through this process. Although, we still need to hold it with Socratic humility, the recognition that we may be wrong.

**Jerry:** Going back to a point you made earlier about the dialogue or conversation I have with God, it is between a person, God, and another person, Jerry. You have talked about a dividing line- they are two separate people. However, in the overall frame of the book, repeated in various contexts, I am told we are part of God. God is in us. And we are in God. It is as if we are a kind of differentiated part of God. The God as we know God is a differentiated part of the total divine reality, or you might say the personal manifestation of divine reality.

Part of the equipment you bring to reading the book is not just reason and a kind of syllogistic sense of laying out arguments, but part of the equipment for understanding is the God in you. The divine element, the divine receptors and perceptors that are in you.

**Richard:** That's a good point. There is a quote from the book on page 91 that speaks to this. God is talking about how human beings are a differentiated element of God, and God says,

> **"There is still a difference between your voice and Mine, since you are a specific manifestation of Me and I am in fact a specific manifestation of Myself."**

A very interesting line! And this can be related to our whole discussion about revelation. The God who speaks to you is a specific manifestation of a greater whole.

**Jerry:** Of this larger whole.

**Richard:** Yes, and the God we are hearing in the book is one specific manifestation of this larger whole, speaking through Jerry Martin.

**Jerry:** As God is speaking to this other manifestation, the reader is a third manifestation. To the extent that we have divine eyes, we have a very good chance of seeing the truth. That is a good place to conclude.

**Richard:** Yes, very good—an encouraging conclusion. Next time, perhaps, we can focus on what God says about *why* God has delivered this revelation to you.

# 3. The Purpose of the Revelation

**Dr. Jerry L. Martin** What are we pursuing today?

**Dr. Richard Oxenberg** Today I thought we would focus on the purpose of the revelation you received. If we look at the various revelatory communications that God has made over the course of history, each one seems to be in response to a problem that needs to be addressed. For instance, the Old Testament revelations seem to be a response to corruptions associated with paganism. Can we articulate the problem that the revelation you received is given in response to?

**Jerry:** It is not a single problem. Throughout the book what is new and surprising or leading messages are any number of things one might pick up. At the beginning, God told me, "I want you to tell My story." At first I said, "Well, hasn't it been told already?" I was thinking mainly, given my background, of the Bible. God responded,

> "Yes, but it needs to be told again and in a different way."

Two reasons. One is the state of religiosity in the world today. The old religions are falling apart; some do not have the authority they used to, and many people are turning away from religion altogether and into various modes of spirituality. Anything goes! A rigid religious framework is no longer adequate. "Anything goes" is not a serious spiritual life at all. So, that is one problem. The other is that a lot has happened since the ancient scriptures. God has evolved since then. That was a very surprising concept to me at the time I was first given this assignment.

Then as I began to look at the world's spiritual situation, if you ask what I take personally to be the main new thrust, it is that God is really, really personal. This means that God actually wants things of us, and that God, in other words, cares about our lives and our actions in a personal way, like a parent for a child or a friend, or one good friend for another. God really, really loves us. Love is not a metaphor or some analogical concept. God really loves us. One of the most shocking statements to me at the time was God telling me,

### "Get more anthropomorphic."

Everything we are taught by the philosophers and high theology is to get less anthropomorphic. It is an understandable impulse. We understand God is not walking around on two legs even though various religions and myths have scenes like that. The old man in the sky, with a big, long beard, might sit on a throne—that kind of anthropomorphism. But I take it that we are made in God's image, which means that God is a lot like us. We are theomorphic. We have loves, and God has loves. We want certain things to happen, and so does God.

I was led to read the ancient scriptures and various traditions and to pray about them. The story was that God was acting in different ways through the different cultures, including some that do not have current major religions- the ancient Egyptians, for example. I prayed with the question, "God, what were You up to with the Egyptians, the Israelites, the Chinese, and so on?" There is a big story there of God acting in different ways, showing different sides of the divine self through different cultures—and developing in the process.

**Richard:** I find the whole idea of getting more anthropomorphic a bit paradoxical—because the book suggests that our conception of the nature or form of the human being itself has to broaden and change. So, though we may need to get more anthropomorphic in our conception of God, at the same time we need to expand or modify our conception of the anthropomorphic itself. There is a strange dialectic between God and the human being in the book, both of whom are not only evolving together but evolving in dependency upon one another.

**Jerry:** God is reacting.

**Richard:** Yes, one of the more enigmatic quotes from the book is when God says that the human response to God, "**is at the heart of My being.**" How do you understand that?

**Jerry:** I wondered, "If You are God, why does it matter to You, this eternal self-sufficient being, whether human beings pay any attention or not?" I say, "Is human recognition important to You?"
"**Yes,**" God replies, "**it is essential to My being.**"
So it is a deeply cooperative, interactive relationship. When we respond to God in a particular way, that makes God aware of the aspect of the divine to which we are responding. So when the Chinese, for example, respond to the ultimate in terms of a kind of cosmic harmony, God notices that is right and becomes more of a cosmic harmony, rises to that recognition in much the way that happens with human beings. You find yourself seen as the leader of a group, and you realize leadership abilities you did not know, and you actually become a better leader as you now recognize that capacity in yourself. So there are those sorts of interactions between us and God.

**Richard:** I am still trying to understand the intimate connection between God and human beings as the book presents it, which I have come to think of as the "participatory" nature of God. The God who is revealed in this book is a God who is fully engaged and participating in the human evolutionary process. God is engaged, not only in the sense of being united with it in some sense, but also caring about it. God needs this evolution to take place in order to fulfill God's *own* longings, needs, and desires. So there is a constant dialectical process going on between humanity and God.

**Jerry:** Yes, right down to the life of the individual.

**Richard:** Right down to the life of the individual. And this is anthropomorphic in one way, and not anthropomorphic in another, because none of us can be united with all other people in the way that God speaks of being united. If we try to envision what such a being would be like, we don't get a picture of a human being.

But getting back to the purpose of the revelation, on page 358 of the book, God says,

> **"You stand on the threshold of a new spiritual era, a new axial age."**

What do you understand that to mean? What is this new Axial Age that we are entering upon?

**Jerry:** We stand on the verge of a new era of spiritual development, something like a new Axial Age. What was the original Axial Age? It was a term put forth by the philosopher Karl Jaspers in the late 1940s to designate the remarkable time in human history when, within a period of about a 500-year span, give or take, religious figures crop up like Confucius and the Buddha, Moses, and Jesus (though they are pretty far apart), Socrates and other wisdom figures in different cultures, transforming the human understanding of the meaning of life and the universe, engaging in a much larger and deeper understanding than ever before. It is a remarkable transition in human consciousness. In some way, analogous to that remarkable, transformative step forward in human consciousness, God says we are on the verge of a similar step forward. This transition seems to be connected with what I learned reading the different scriptures and finding out what God was up to, what is true in each, or what they got wrong, overemphasized, or neglected. It is not simply an endorsement of every religion that came along, but rather we come to understand what God was actually trying to achieve in this or that venue of human culture. Once you start thinking about the divine, not in terms of my religion, your religion, this religion, that religion, ones that are alive, ones that are dead, as if God is contained within the frame of religion, you start thinking beyond those frames. It is not that God stands outside of all that in some abstract universe, but that God is showing Godself differentially through the different religions. That is really a dramatic new way of understanding the divine.

**Richard:** And this, then, led to the Theology Without Walls project that you began.

**Jerry:** In light of this God experience through the different cultures, I was told to start a new theological project called Theology Without Walls. I have done that, and it has received considerable interest.

**Richard:** There does seem to be an opening of mind in this direction. At one point in the book God says that the ultimate goal of reality is "**to create the many and to pull them back into the one.**" And in another place God says, "**the point of reality is to produce a complex, integrated whole diffused with spirit, reflecting a fully developed God.**" The Theology Without Walls project seems an attempt to do just this with respect to religion itself—to integrate the religious visions of the different religions while, at the same time, acknowledging and even honoring their genuine differences.

**Jerry:** Yes. They are genuinely different. There are people who like to say—I think it makes them feel better if they can say—all the religions say the same thing. Yes, but only if you iron them out and get rid of all the wrinkles. In the full body of reality, they are very different. In articulated forms, they are different in the very ways most important to the participants in those religions. They would not be happy to have this ironed out version so that the Buddhist is saying the same thing as the Southern Baptist and vice versa.

The vision God is giving me is of enormous diversity and particularity. The particulars never disappear in some kind of universal scheme or, as if once we put things in the blender, they will all look alike. It is quite the opposite. It is a very complex but orchestrated working toward unity- as though you had several different bands come together. At first, they are discordant. You don't want them all to play exactly alike, but they need to play in ways that complement one another.

**Richard:** In ways that harmonize with one another—to, in a sense, make a greater whole than each can be by itself. One of the metaphors you've used to express this is that of the different pieces of a puzzle. Each piece is different from the others, but they can be put together into a greater whole. Doing this does not homogenize them all into the same piece. Rather, their very differences allow them to fit together in a way that makes for a more complete whole. This is one of the major thrusts of the revelation you've received. God is saying that now I am revealing Myself as the singular force behind all of human spirituality, despite its great diversity.

If we were to embrace this, it would radically change the way we approach religious difference. Instead of asking ourselves which of the religions is right, we would now ask what is right about each of the religions. If the religions of the world would adopt this way of

## THE PURPOSE OF THE REVELATION

thinking, it would change their understanding of both themselves and the other religions. And this itself might move humanity higher up the spiritual ladder.

**Jerry:** Yes. Exactly. How wonderfully framed! I ask at one point, "Does this mean the old religions will have to fade away?" No, not at all. God actually uses the metaphor of a division of labor. "There can be a division of labor." We *could* all do the same thing, but people are needed for various aspects of the divine. You need people like Buddhist monks who go off and do nothing but meditate, but that is not the whole of the world's business. You also need people—in fact, the task given to the ancient people of Israel—to be partners with God in history. You need people doing that. You need people like Dorothy Day worried about feeding the poor. There are a lot of things to be done. There are many aspects of God to be actualized. You need that diversity to continue, and it is perfectly fine. What is new is that each one, Dorothy Day, the Baptists, the Buddhists, the Hindu, and the Jew, will realize that they are not the only story. What they are doing, which may be what God exactly wants them to do, is nevertheless not the only divine task or the only aspect of the divine reality.

**Richard:** This gets expressed by God on page 355 of the book:

> "The same theological truth can be celebrated and lived in different ways. The division of labor (among the different religions) can even continue, with people selecting the vocation that fits their talents or history or calling, but understanding it in a new way, not as the exclusive path, but as an essential path contributing to the whole."

That is a wonderful quote.

**Jerry:** Yes. That sums it up. There, God sums it up for me.

**Richard:** In thinking about what is at the core of your revelation, I came up with three major points the book makes that all seem to relate to one another. One is that God is fully participatory in the creation. God is not standing off somewhere, observing it all, unaffected by what is going on. God is fully invested in our cares and concerns, and even our suffering. In fact, God makes a big point of saying that God suffers with us.

**Jerry:** Yes. That is almost the essential truth in the whole book. When we suffer, God suffers. When we are going the wrong way, God suffers like a loving parent. God suffers in these many ways when tragedy strikes us or when we go wrong. That is a way in which God's destiny does depend on our action. God cannot be felicitous unless we are doing well and living well.

**Richard:** And it is the other way around too, isn't it? We suffer *because* God suffers. In other words, the forces that make for suffering are inherent to the nature of God and, thus, are at the core of *both* God's *and* our suffering. We have to wrestle with these forces because they are part of what reality is, part of what God is. So, our suffering is God's suffering, and God's suffering is our suffering. We have to deal with it together.

**Jerry:** Yes. We are all enmeshed. I had not thought of flipping it that way. But that sounds right. That is the implication.

**Richard:** So, this is one big point the book makes, about the participatory nature of God.

**Jerry:** Yes. That is crucial.

## THE PURPOSE OF THE REVELATION

**Richard:** A second point is the new understanding of the world's religions the book presents. On the one hand, it is not an exclusivist understanding, with one religion standing up and saying this is the one and only truth. On the other hand, it is not a dismissive understanding, saying that since one of them cannot be the truth, therefore none of them have any truth. It is a new conception of the religions that sees each as divinely inspired and as providing a path toward the divine, and each as having a role to play in human spirituality.

**Jerry:** The challenge for an individual is defined by discerning which of those religious paths or other paths—philosophical, psychological, or whatever—makes the divine most accessible to that person. It might be the religion they were born into, but it might not. They might be called to a different religion or to one of these alternative paths to be philosophical, to be some inspired poet, or just to help people, to give a life of service without thinking a lot about a theological dimension, just be a giving person. There might be any number of things. The challenge for the individual is to figure out what does God want me to do? And where do I find God? Do I find God here or there?

I had experiences when I was going through this, with a hypersensitive spirituality, of going into a synagogue and feeling the divine palpable. Almost as if I walked into a wall of just the divine. I had the opposite experience in a downtown church. I went and just was curious about this space. I knew nothing about religion until God talked to me, and I started paying attention. In this church, I am looking at the walls; what do the posters say? What is going on here? I suddenly felt I was suffocating. There was no oxygen in this room. I literally raced out of the room and back to the street. Those are just personal reactions. But you can explore for yourself where you find the divine accessible and what is most deeply meaningful for your life.

I do not report it in the book, but I gave a subsequent talk at the Won Institute for Buddhist Studies. Won Buddhism is a 20th-century Japanese inspiration to people who founded this particular branch. I delayed the invitation for a while because I thought Buddhists do not believe in God. Isn't this going to seem very wrong to them or a very low-level of spirituality, too literalistic? But the person inviting me had heard me give a talk at AAR and persisted. I went and in fact we had a great discussion.

One story that came out of that was they just hired a Jewish psychologist. I asked her, how did you end up with the Won Buddhist institute? Well, she was in downtown Philadelphia. It started raining, and she ran into the nearest building to get out of the rain. It turned out to be the Won institute of Buddhist Spirituality. It just came upon her: This is where I belong. I have come to think you need to pay attention to moments like that. You could think, "Oh, well. That is silly. It was just a place out of the rain." On the other hand, you learn more if you trust it. She did and she ended up working with them. This is her career and perhaps her calling. It is not just that there are a number of religions, each doing their own thing. We as individuals have a relationship to those religious doors we can open or not open, or we can happen to discover in our lives one door that is already open and waiting for us.

**Richard:** The book suggests that we are not merely to respect one another's religions in a political sense, but that we should respect one another's religions as having revelatory significance.

**Jerry:** Yes. And, as a result, being able to learn from one another if we so choose. I do not find here any mandate to people that they have to go study all the religions. It is perfectly fine just to do your thing. Just be aware that it is not the only divine avenue.

**Richard:** It seems to me that as the different religions begin to adopt this view of themselves, the hard edges of the religions will begin

## THE PURPOSE OF THE REVELATION

to soften. It is not simply that there will now be opportunities for an individual to hop from one religion to another, but that the religions themselves will modify their understanding of themselves, recognizing that, though they each have their particular focus, their focus is but one focus within a much greater whole. And this will change their understanding of the meaning of their own religion as well.

**Jerry:** As long as they are able to keep their focus, there is nothing against their bringing, right into their midst, the other points of view. A Christian congregation, for example, can bring in somebody to talk about Gandhi's spirituality or Buddhism. We can study. We can all read the poetry of Rumi, the Islamic poet, and go back then to our Methodist worship because that is mainly what we are doing. It is a Methodist church without walls, you might say.

**Richard:** The third point that came to me from the book, related to everything else we've discussed, is what we might think of as the "integrative" nature of God. We live in a world of enormous diversity; it sometimes seems astonishing to me that reality is capable of such diversity. Yet, all this diversity somehow emerges from a fundamental Unity, which allows for the possibility that this diversity can harmonize with itself. And the book suggests that the pursuit of this harmony is, in some sense, the essential goal of life. By establishing harmonious relations with God, nature, and one another, we are best able to achieve a satisfying life.

**Jerry:** Meanwhile, our job is just to do our thing. It reminds me of the story of the guy who is a tuba player in a symphony orchestra. One time, he got sick. They are doing Aida, and since he is sick, he goes out and sits in the audience and listens to the music. He says to his friend afterward, "It was amazing. You know, the part where I'm just going oompa oompa oompa? The whole orchestra is playing, da da de DAH- the grand march." The whole of Aida is there. He just never had any idea. Nevertheless, he is still a tuba player, and his job is to go back and play the tuba. If he does his job, then we get Aida. The musical metaphor seems to come up often in the book because harmony is a powerful metaphor in itself. It allows one to appreciate the full diversity. The particulars all have to stay there. The tuba has to do its oompa, oompa, oompa; meanwhile, all these other instruments are doing their particular thing. Yet it does make a meaningful whole.

**Richard:** And this can be related to the discussion in the book about the ego, which the book speaks of as "separative." Our ego is what separates us from everything else. This is necessary, but the danger is that we can become so wrapped up in our separative ego that, for instance, the tuba player comes to think that his playing the tuba is all that is important in the world, and that the orchestra exists merely to provide the occasion for his tuba playing.

**Jerry:** Yes. When I pray about what is wrong with the ego, I am told there is a good ego and a bad ego. Or a good sense and a bad sense. In the good sense, you need an ego that is part of your equipment, your engine, and your armor for dealing with a difficult world. You need self-esteem and a firm sense of your own purpose and commitments. In the bad sense, ego is separatist. When it is separatist and rebellious, it is as if the tuba player said, "Well, I am not going to pay attention to the score because I could just make the tuba louder and more dominant and do all kinds of stuff that will drown the others out." It is that ego that is completely self-preoccupied and does not see itself as part of a whole of any kind, part of interpersonal relations, or anything else of that kind, that we have to avoid.

**Richard:** A good quote that expresses this is on page 148. God says,

> "The material world—the senses, ego, and so forth—is deceptively powerful. It is easy for it to

## THE PURPOSE OF THE REVELATION

**seem like the only thing that matters, in fact like the only thing that is really real."**

One of the big aims of spirituality is to get us beyond the ego, to recognize our connection with what stands beyond the ego without doing away with the ego.

**Jerry:** Right. But ego, like the tuba, has a particular role. To help us navigate the world. To give us some defenses against the slings and arrows that might be showered upon us and help us stand for what we are standing for and pursue our projects with some degree of single-mindedness. But it must remain limited.

The other part of that quote is about the physical world, which seems very real in one's own physiology, one's own body, one's own bodily desires, and the worldly goods that we are surrounded with, as well as the worldly dangers. They are assertively real. And so it is very easy to think that is the total level of reality. It is a lot of reality. What God told me cuts in between two points of view. Because there are other people who want to say that the world is something like an illusion. However, I am told, "If it is a mirage, it is a mirage you can drink water from." It is a completely real thing however you label it metaphysically.

**Richard:** In this context the book goes into a discussion of sacrifice, because sacrifice and surrender are what the ego needs to do in order to overcome its intensive self-involvement. It is through sacrifice and surrender that it can enter into a relationship with what stands beyond it—and this, I suppose, is the essential meaning of love.

**Jerry:** Yes. Love always involves an element of surrender. Not just pushing the other person around or trying to use them for your own desires, emotional needs, or physical lust, but to surrender a lot of that to the good of the other and to the preciousness of the other. Our relation to God has those elements too, and our relation to other high ideals—things people fight and die for, things people sacrifice for. I know a guy who takes food to the people in India. As it happens, he is a deep introvert, and he hates having to go to India and hates doing all this, the mosquitos, and all the horrors, with often wretched conditions. That is hard for him to bear, but he feels called to do this, and so he surrenders to that very uncomfortable call. That is a lot of life. It seems to be essential to our relation to God.

That is why I always pray, "Thy will be done." Most people pray, "Give me this; give me that." It is like, "God, let my will be done." To the extent you are doing that, you are not related to God as a divine being at all but as a kind Santa Clause or fairy godmother.

**Richard:** And I suppose God's will, as it gets expressed in the book, is ultimately the will to—well, I call it 'integration'—but ultimately this means to create love, to recognize the forces of *dis*-integration, and then deal with them in such a way as to bring them into harmony with one another, in whatever manner this can be done in our world. So—as so many of the religions tell us—love is the ultimate purpose.

Maybe this is a good place to bring this session to a close. What we are planning to do next is talk about the nature of God as revealed in the book

**Jerry:** You are doing a wonderful job of pulling out these themes and these ideas from the book and articulating them with great clarity and aptness and crispness. That is impressive and very useful.

**Richard:** I enjoy doing it, and it has helped me. Preparing to do these talks with you has forced me to dig more deeply into the book and think about it more. As I do, I am seeing more in it than I had before.

**Jerry:** That is what happens. That is why one reads a worthwhile book more than once.

# 4. The Nature of the Divine Reality

**Dr. Jerry L. Martin** I am glad to have a chance to continue our dialogue on *God: An Autobiography*. What are we talking about today?

**Dr. Richard Oxenberg** So far, we have been discussing your experiences with God and the purpose of the revelation you received. I thought today we would focus on the nature of God as presented in the book. The understanding of God presented in the book is rather different from some of the standard ways we tend to think about God.

**Jerry:** It surprised me when God presented Godself this way.

**Richard:** There is a line in the book where God says,

> "Now we need a new systematic revelation, from bottom to top, almost to start over again—with a (new) Genesis, one might say, with a new gospel of John. And a new philosophical understanding of God. The old one was only partly inspired and contains too much of the arrogance of human reason."

So, let's focus on the new Genesis.

**Jerry:** Yes. What you just quoted was a very early prayer before we got to the new Genesis. I was trying to get oriented. What on Earth are we doing here? What is God doing with me? That was before the new Genesis actually occurred.

**Richard:** It might be interesting to read the creation story as we find it in the old Genesis and then compare it to the creation as presented in your book. Here is the very beginning of how the Book of Genesis begins in the Revised Standard Version of the Bible:

> "In the beginning, God created the Heavens and the Earth. The Earth was without form and void, and darkness was upon the face of the deep; and the Spirit of God was moving over the face of the waters. And God said, "Let there be light," and there was light. And God saw that the light was good; and God separated the light from the darkness. God called the light Day, and the darkness he called Night. And there was evening, and there was morning one day."

**Jerry:** Beautiful, quite magisterial.

**Richard:** Yes. It presents the image of a God who is fully in command of Godself and the creation. This contrasts rather sharply with the image of the creation that we get from your book.

Let's look at the creation story as we read it in your book. This is God speaking:

> "I am in the midst of Nothing. I don't know who or what I am—I am like a baby in a womb. I hear nothing, see nothing—because there is nothing. I feel alone, very alone, except that I don't yet know what alone means. I feel growing strength, and Myself being drawn toward the light, just

> a glimmer at the 'edge.' I am in a kind of 'pain,' like stretching aching muscles. Suddenly, it is as if I punch my arms and legs through the sides of a bag I'm in. It is like an explosion. In a split second, fragments are zooming out in all directions. I am at a throbbing, pulsing center. I am not sure what's happening... I scramble to take control, to provide order."

These are two very different images of 'the beginning'! What do you make of that?

**Jerry:** At the time, I was quite shocked because I grew up with Genesis. There is no other conception, as you say, of God or creation that was remotely like this. And it seemed too anthropomorphic, and when I ask about that, God says that kind of language is the only way to communicate what this was like. You have to reach for some language that we can use of a God who seemed to be coming into existence simultaneously with the world coming into existence.

There is that sense that, before, God was in Nothingness, and the Nothingness does not seem to be quite nothing completely. At one point I said, "Maybe it is like a pregnant nothingness- a nothingness full of potentiality?" God responded, "Well, okay, that is an okay way to put it."

Then God and the world explode together. The Big Bang and the world expanded in a microsecond. God noticed that the divine role is somehow to orchestrate this. It is as though you find yourself in front of a one hundred and fifty piece orchestra and they start tuning up and you realize, suddenly, I have to give direction.

**Richard:** That itself is an interesting image. It suggests at first that God is somehow separate from everything else. When you say that it is like you are in the middle of an orchestra, and the orchestra is tuning up, and you are the conductor, and you have to somehow get the orchestra to tune up properly—well, the conductor is not the rest of the orchestra. There is a distinction between the conductor and the orchestra.

Also, the creation story in the book almost sounds like a description of a birth. There is a kind of womb—you use the word pregnant—it is almost as if God suddenly explodes and bursts out of this womb, not quite knowing what is going on. God says, on page 73,

> **"Out of Nothingness I erupted, 'created' Myself. At that point, I was just pure energy, pure creative force, pure Being, Being itself. Space and time were created as a result of My Being."**

The God depicted here does not sound like someone in complete control. This is a process God is subject to, and the process explodes out at some point, very much like the Big Bang. God says,

> **"The physical universe spun out of Me by My overflowing. I am the to-be of all things. I was not yet a Person. I was not yet self-aware. I was amorphous energy flowing out radically in all directions."**

What a difference between this and the Genesis story! What this seems to be saying is that the personhood of God somehow crystalizes out of this explosion. If God is like the conductor of an orchestra, it is a conductor who does not quite know how he or the orchestra got there. Or, to put it another way, it is like an orchestra in which one element of the orchestra suddenly becomes aware of itself, and then aware of the orchestra as outside of itself, and then aware of its need to create some kind of order within the orchestra.

**Jerry:** That is one aspect of the picture. But the other aspect is that this physical universe that is exploding like the Big Bang, or like a newborn coming out with arms and legs kicking, is also the world. It is also the world. It is as if God is the mind of this vast, exploding body and has to figure out what to do with these flailing arms and legs or with these extraordinary thrusts outward of energy and mass. God is trying to figure it out.

It is odd. It is a double aspect that is constant through the book, the way in which God is the world and is us and the way in which we encounter God. God is not just us and not just the world but presents a personal side. In other ways, we can be participatory in the divine. Those aspects are always there, somewhat paradoxically. It is paradoxical, given how we ordinarily relate to physical objects around us.

**Richard:** So, is Genesis wrong? Is there or is there not some truth to the way Genesis presents the creation story? Are we going to say that the author of Genesis just got it wrong, and the account of creation in your book is what really happened? What would you say about that?

**Jerry:** That is not a question that I have asked myself. I tend to be trusting with regard to revelations and assume that they are each telling us something. I do not think that implies one has to hammer them into one story and ask what exactly is the right story? These are both rather metaphorical and majestic presentations. How is God going to communicate creation in a way that we are going to find it easy to grasp?

I pray about Genesis later. God is not trying to correct the story, but just provided an interpretation of key lines. The dialogue was in the spirit of here are the truths articulated maybe differently from some particular theological tradition, but it did contain truths. There was something said about a translation of some of the terms—that God "fluttered over the waters" like a bird over its young. One does have to be sensitive to these images, to these nuances of language. It is almost like reading poetry. What I was told is that God now wants us to understand certain things about the creation.

**Richard:** Perhaps it's possible—and this is a point made in the book overall—to see both of these stories as different aspects of a greater truth, and to think of each of them as having their own spiritual value. An interesting question to consider is how each of these stories might have significance from a spiritual point of view, how each might be saying something spiritually important for us to hear. Another thing that comes up in the creation story in the book, and that is rather shocking and curious, is God's description of being lonely.

**Jerry:** It becomes something of a persistent theme. In the next chapter, God is amazed when life appears, which seems somewhat surprising and delightful to God, even the moss and the really low, swampy stuff. "It is all wonderful," God says. It is just wonderful in itself how life emerges and develops in its splendiferous forms. Also, God starts feeling, "Hey! I have company!" God says that molecules and atoms are like centers of life at a basic level. They are not just dead matter; there is a kind of pulsing life right down to the molecules. Nevertheless, that is not enough to make one not feel lonely. It is not enough for meaningful companionship and interaction. Whereas, when you start getting life, organic life, that changes.

**Richard:** It seems to be this loneliness within God that is driving God forward. This is the hunger that is motivating God to do whatever God is doing. Loneliness implies a kind of privation, a need. So, we get an image of a God who first becomes aware of Godself as in dire need of something beyond what God is at that moment. This need motivates God's creative activity as well as God's endeavor to be in relationship with human beings.

**Jerry:** Yes. It is a very great need. There is a reading of the Adam and Eve story in the book where God takes the story in its own terms and asks, "What does that story tell you?" That is a story where God first feels it is possible just to walk among the creatures. Then God thinks Adam needs a human partner, not just God, and so Eve is created. And then God finds Adam loves Eve more than he loves God, and God becomes neglected. Adam and Eve know they are disobeying and that this is wrong, and so they hide in their shame. They violated a rule, and they are now aware of their nakedness. Before, they were childlike. In this way, God discovers that it is not possible for God to relate to human beings in that way—playing with them in the Garden of Eden. God cannot relate to them in that simple way.

**Richard:** I've never been exactly sure how to read that—it seems as if God is being, not just childlike, but even a bit childish.

**Jerry:** God is somewhat like a child. God has not yet learned how to relate to people and the world, just as a child does not necessarily know what the limbs will do. Children at first do not know there is a difference between themselves and the mother. It is just a blur, them and the world and their own body is one blur, and it slowly gets clarified. God is not quite that elementary, but it is something analogous to that.

**Richard:** The book tells us a number of times that God is coming into self-awareness. This is one of the most enigmatic elements of the book. God is coming into self-awareness along with, and in response to, human awareness of God.

**Jerry:** God says a self requires another self. The philosophy of Hegel has a famous section arguing something like that. You cannot know yourself as a self unless you encounter another self, and that brings your selfhood forward in presenting yourself to the other. Then both selves are bringing their selfhood forward and reacting. So, the two selfhoods grow together in the encounter and in the interaction.

At first, like the child, you do not know yourself. If you are the only thing around, the concept of a self does not even quite make sense. Myself is distinct from what? But if you have another self, then, they are them, I am me, and even though there is this underlying sense in which they are, in some sense, also me, we are encountering each other as selves, and as different, and as able to react to one another in different ways, and therefore able to develop in that interaction.

**Richard:** Yes, but it is not simply that God is becoming aware of God's relation to human selves. God is discovering what God is *through* the human discovery of what God is. There is a co-evolution taking place, which is completely different from the idea of God we are accustomed to in the Western tradition. It is so different, in fact, that it almost calls into question whether the word "God" is fully appropriate. What we are calling "God" here is coevolving with everything else. God's evolution is dependent upon human evolution, so that the God who speaks in this book is united with human beings in a way that we might almost call organic. God's development and human development are entirely intermeshed. The human beings are not just dependent upon God, but God is dependent upon the human beings. Am I getting this right?

**Jerry:** That is exactly right. That is very analogous to human development. Richard is a good teacher. How does Richard know that Richard is a good teacher? How does Richard actualize that side of Richard? How does that side of Richard come into being? It is by having classes and students and interacting with students' responses. One trait after another that human beings have are brought about by interactions among people. They are recognized by the persons themselves as traits of themselves by other people labeling them. They say you are a leader, or you are a thinker, and then you recognize. That is right; I never thought of myself that way! It is very much like that.

God develops by discovering with the ancient people of Israel a lawgiver side. Before, God had just sent people ethical intuitions or ethical prompts like natural sympathy, a discomfort when betraying one's friends, and so forth. In the context of interacting with the people of Israel, these ethical prompts get codified. God lays down a covenant. We need to have rules, and people need to be told what these rules are. It needs to be somewhat systematic, and so we get the Ten Commandments. This is not how God relates to people in any other culture. There is no other covenant. There is no other Ten Commandments, though there are rules, but not in this mode of divine commandments.

**Richard:** There is a passage in the book where God says referring to this, "Well, I was a little bit overly concerned with ritual in those days, but you have to remember, I was young."

**Jerry:** God was young and we were young, and so a natural place to begin the relationship was through rituals, so God was punctilious about rituals. They are just behavior, not rituals, unless they are done right.

**Richard:** I've puzzled over the idea of God being young. If we attend to what modern physics has to say, the universe is about 14 billion years old, and God's interaction with the Israelites occurred only a few thousand years ago, so in what sense was God young? It seems to me that God can be thought of as young here only if we understand the God who speaks in the book as tied to human development in a way that is very different from the way we think of God in the Western tradition.

Here is a quote from page 140 of the book that relates to this. God says,

> "It is not (only) creatures who are imperfect. I am too. I need this development in order to become more perfect, more fulfilled. I need it and human beings do as well."

And in another passage you say to God, "So one dimension of your story is the personal co-partnering," and God responds,

> "Not just one dimension—the crucial dimension."

One question that emerges for me from this way of thinking of God is: In what sense can this God be an object of worship? If God is just figuring Godself out, if God is co-developing with human beings, if God is making mistakes, if God is not altogether sure of who God is or the plan God is enacting, what makes God an object of devotion?

When one prays to God, worships God, there is a sense in which you are looking for someone you can count on, rely on, trust to provide guidance, security, and greater wisdom. But if this God is just figuring things out along with us, where does the God who we can worship come in?

**Jerry:** I have not myself thought of being worthy of worship as essential to the concept of God. So that throws me off a little. What can I worship? That is a different question from anything I was pursuing here. Obedience does come up and something like deference which is analogized to the young person deferring to an elder. A gentleman may defer in certain contexts to a lady and let her get on the lifeboat first as a recognition of their statuses or roles in life. You might defer to your rabbi or priest. You might obey your sergeant or your boss. Or the person who has the savvy to get you out of a jam. Those relationships are not perfection, but relations of fitting deference. But there is still the larger question. There is a young God setting out the Ten Commandments. Why should we follow them?

## THE NATURE OF THE DIVINE REALITY

There is other ancient wisdom literature and, of course, it turns out that God is behind those too. Still, why should we pay any attention to any of them if they come from a God finding His way? The drama of our mutual development is part of the answer. It is as if the orchestra conductor is trying to figure out the piece. We are going to do a better job if we are all paying attention to the orchestra conductor than if we each just do what we feel like doing with our own instruments. God is following a telos, an ultimate aim to the universe that has not yet emerged. But God is getting glimmers along the way. God is following those glimmers and is learning more precisely by interacting with us, and we are following God who is taking us forward.

**Richard:** So, as I was reading through the book, all these questions were in my mind: How can God be lonely? How can God have been born out of Nothingness? In what way is this a God that one can turn to and worship? In what way does this God address the spiritual urge of human beings? And, for me, this only started to make sense when I put it into the context of what you call in the book "the God beyond God."

The God beyond God is the God out of which this God emerges. If we ask what the ultimate reality is, or what is at the foundation of reality, it is not this God. It is the God beyond God. It is the God beyond God from which this God arises and that is the ontological basis of this God. In this respect, the God who speaks in the book is more an exalted creature than the Creator.

And what we seem to be getting in the first book of Genesis is something of an amalgam of this God and the God beyond God. Perhaps such an amalgam is appropriate because, as we are told in the book, this God is just one face of the God beyond God.

**Jerry:** Yes. The God beyond God in the form of the God entering and creating this world is sometimes analogized to an actor playing a role. Richard Burton enters the role of Hamlet, and then he is

Hamlet. If you think of that stage as the real world, then he is living out the Hamlet or the God of that world and then can step back and is not exhausted. There is more to the God beyond God than just God in this world, in this incarnation in this world. However, it is not quite right to say the God beyond God is more real. It certainly starts there, but that God is mainly a potentiality that has to be actualized in the God in this world and, I am told, many other worlds.

**Richard:** So it is the God beyond God to whom the word eternal would apply, not the God of this world. The God of this world is temporal, developing, has a past and a future, and is working toward that future, very much like a big human being. But it is the God beyond God that is—to use a phrase from Paul Tillich—the 'ground of being.'

This 'ground of being' is not, as Aristotle would have expressed it, pure actuality, but more a pure potentiality in need of actualization. So the creation—both of God and the universe—arises out of the need of the God beyond God to self-actualize. And there are any number of ways in which this self-actualization can occur. To refer again to the orchestra analogy, there are more and less beautiful pieces of music that the orchestra can play. It can play its music in a harmonious way or in a very discordant way painful to the ears. Our task, as members of the orchestra, is to try to make beautiful music.

**Jerry:** I would add one qualification, it is not that this is just a need of the God beyond God as a privation, but it is also God's job. There is a good to be done that God is being called to do and so to create these worlds. These are whole worlds with meaningful lives being lived on them and the meaning is in the worlds. It is not in God sitting back satisfying a need to have toys. God is orchestrating for a purpose. The purpose is something like the meaningful dramas that are lived out in each world. That fits with the passage you read about God co-partnering in our lives and the God beyond God entering the world in order to co-partner with our lives. So, add that to the picture.

**Richard:** Maybe in our next discussion we can explore a little bit more fully the notion of the God beyond God. In Western theology this is sometimes called the God*head*. Maybe this will help us gain a fuller understanding of how your revelation is related to the human spiritual urge.

**Jerry:** We will move in that direction, Richard.

# 5. The Big Picture

**Dr. Jerry L. Martin** What is our topic for today?

**Dr. Richard Oxenberg** Hi Jerry. Today I thought we would try to get an overall metaphysical picture of what God is telling us in the book.

**Jerry:** The big picture.

**Richard:** Yes, the big picture—I think that when you look at the whole picture things come together in a way that they don't when you look at it piecemeal.
   One of the interesting aspects of your revelations is that they seem, at one and the same time, both familiar and very unfamiliar. The God who speaks to you is in many ways reminiscent of the biblical God, and professes to be the God of the Bible. Yet, at the same time, the picture we get of the universe and of the nature of God is really quite different from the standard Western conception of the Almighty God who is in control of everything. And there are many implications for spiritual life that arise from these differences. By looking at the big picture, I think we'll be able to see these implications more clearly.
   So, what is the big picture? To lay it out in outline form, we might first discuss what the book calls "the God beyond God,"

which I take to be the ultimate reality, the 'ground of being,' out of which everything else arises. Then we might look at what I have come to think of as 'the emergent God,' the God that emerges out of the God beyond God and who is the principal speaker to you in your book. Then we might talk about the general teleological view we get from these—what is the overall spiritual aim or purpose?

**Jerry:** That is right. The God of our world is the emergent God, as you call it. There is the question of what is the point of it all. What is the point? What is the purpose?

**Richard:** Also, what is the message that we should take from it? What is the takeaway? Let us begin, then, with the God beyond God. The God beyond God first shows up as an idea on page 73. God here is speaking of God's own emergence. Prior to that emergence, we read,

> **"There was a Self, timeless, without reflection, still and at peace, like calm waters, lucid, not nothing, but not something either."**

I take this as a description of what is later in the book called the God beyond God.

**Jerry:** Yes. That is very good reading to pick that up as the earliest mention of the God beyond God. I was puzzled because the story of God, in a way, starts with creation. But there is the puzzlement of what was before creation. What was God doing then? I was told that God was not a nothing, and was in a kind of peace, calm, but not yet quite a something either.

**Richard:** It resembles in some ways the distinction Meister Eckhart makes between God and the Godhead. We find this distinction in a number of different religions. In Hinduism, for instance, there is a distinction made between Brahman Saguna and Brahman Nirguna; the Brahman with qualities and the Brahman without qualities, where Brahman Nirguna is more fundamental than Brahman Saguna. The God beyond God is the ultimate reality, that out of which everything arises. Let's consider some of the characteristics of the God beyond God.

**Jerry:** Well, there are contexts you have to put this discussion within. One is the multiple worlds that I found very disturbing. There are an infinite number, endless worlds. I had been told so many weird things; this was one too many, and I stopped praying for a while. A God in each world seems to be the implication.

**Richard:** The God beyond God is timeless, but the gods of each of the many worlds are not timeless; they are temporal.

**Jerry:** Right, within the world, it is temporal.

**Richard:** So, we have a picture of an ultimate, timeless reality out of which innumerable temporal realities spring. This makes me think of the vision you saw at the very beginning of your revelational experiences, the image of the fountain.

**Jerry:** Yes. A rising, sparkling, multicolored fountain. A kind of vision, but like a hologram of a fountain.

**Richard:** It is almost as if the God beyond God is the fountain out of which all of this great creativity rises.

**Jerry:** Yes, that is right. The other context, in addition to infinite worlds, is reincarnation.

**Richard:** Yes, the emergent God is, so to speak, an incarnation of the God beyond God. There is a reincarnational quality both to the God beyond God and to us, in that the God beyond God, like ourselves, keeps reincarnating—there is a kind of parallel between the two.

**Jerry:** There is a parallel. It is important to remember that these are not two different gods. It can easily sound as if there is the God of our world and then another, bigger God standing behind it, doing a bigger magic show. In the context of reincarnation, it is like the difference between my self or personality in this world and what you might call my soul, or what is sometimes called the self behind the self. They are not two different selves, but one is myself, navigating the world, and the other is a more divine side, a little more distant, watching my progress in this world.

**Richard:** Not only is the God beyond God not ultimately different from the God of this world and the Gods of all the other worlds, but the God of this world and the Gods of the other worlds are not ultimately different from us. In an ultimate sense, it is all one.

**Jerry:** There is that complication, too. I am constantly told we are both other than and the same as God, and both aspects are essential. God infuses us. God is part of us. We are part of God. At the same time, we are sufficiently different that we can encounter one another, love one another, and have a drama together.

**Richard:** The question that next occurs to me—to follow this out in a logical way—is why does this God beyond God, who is calm and at peace, create anything at all?

We get an answer to this question on page 184, where it says that the potential for all things resides in the God beyond God but that this potential seeks actualization. Here is the quote:

> **"Reality wants to be embodied. In this respect, philosophical traditions that derive from Plato, Aristotle, Plotinus get it wrong. The material**

> **object does not 'fall beneath' the 'perfect' form; it actualizes it."**

There is within the God beyond God, despite its being at peace—or maybe this is part of its peace—a desire to be embodied.

**Jerry:** Peace as having a lot of potentialities. It is not actual.

**Richard:** It wants to produce. It exists as a tremendous creative force out of which arises the incredible diversity we see in the worlds, not just in our world, but within an infinite number of worlds. On some level, though, in spite of all the difficulties encountered in these worlds, it remains, in some sense, at peace.

**Jerry:** Yes. In an ideal mode.

**Richard:** So, we have an ultimate reality that is timeless and eternal, and out of this ultimate reality springs the temporal in an infinite variety of permutations, one of which is our world and the God of our world, who is just one of the many emergent gods of the infinite worlds that go on and on. That is the mega picture.

**Jerry:** That is the biggest picture. I am always uncomfortable with that picture—infinite worlds, infinite gods or embodiments or emergences of the God beyond God. I was happy when this chapter came to an end, and we got back to our world and our God.

**Richard:** One other dimension to the God beyond God we should mention—before we start talking about the emergent God—is expressed on page 318 of the book. At this point, you have come to call the God beyond God, the 'Atman of God.'

**Jerry:** I am borrowing and somewhat changing the Hindu concept of the Atman, something like the soul or the self behind the self.

In the Hindu tradition, or a central strand of it, is that soul that is fully identical with the Brahman, the ultimate reality. Here, it is a little different. The Atman is individual. Your soul always remains individual. So, in addition to Richard, there is the Atman or Soul of Richard. In addition to the God of this world, there is the Atman of God, another term for the God beyond God.

**Richard:** The God of this world tells you to try to feel into what the God beyond God is like. You describe it this way,

> "I get the feeling of benign shelter, as if the thrashing about of the world and of the God of this world needs a container to hold it together and everything is safely enveloped by the Atman of God."

I thought this was a beautiful picture. In spite of all the "whips and scorns of time" we suffer in this world, at an ultimate level, there is peace—benign shelter. The God beyond God is the ultimate safety net. However horrible things might get out here in this messy world, we can come to recognize that there is a benign shelter underlying it all, a shelter that is eternal, that we are all ultimately rooted in, and that is not subject to decay.

**Jerry:** Yes. I assume just as we are both same as and different from the God of this world, we are both same as and different from the Atman of God, the God beyond God, which is, of course, just the other dimension of the God of this world.

**Richard:** This seems to me an important thing to be aware of from a spiritual point of view. One of the things we turn to spirituality for is to put us in touch with something that transcends the hardships and difficulties of this world, something that can provide us a sense of inner peace despite the many troubles we encounter in life.

In one of his epistles, St. Paul speaks of this spiritual peace as "the peace that passes all understanding."

**Jerry:** Good point. It is not like an escape hatch, as though one could run off to the God beyond God. That is not what happens. But one can be at peace in the way that God beyond God is at peace. We are also, in part, identical with the God beyond God, and so we have that peace in our soul, right in the midst of the hurly-burly of our difficult world.

**Richard:** In this context, I think of the image of Jesus sleeping on the boat during the storm. His disciples are in a panic over the storm, and Jesus is sleeping peacefully. They wake him up and say, "Master, Master! We are about to go under!" And Jesus responds, "Oh, ye of little faith!"—the idea being that if they had true faith they would not be panicking. One of the great problems of religion is in reconciling belief in an ultimate goodness, an ultimate peace, with all the hardships and troubles present in our world. Your revelations give us a way of understanding how we might do this.

**Jerry:** It is interesting. This is why I love having a serious reader like you of the book, because I had never made that connection. I variously talked with God, the God of this world, about the problem of suffering, and God never tries to explain suffering away as some apologists of the religions try to do. Suffering is really bad God tells me, but I get a little perspective on it that alleviates the awfulness slightly. The point you are now making had never occurred to me—that there is another viewpoint and another locus in reality that is peaceful amidst all of this.

**Richard:** Let's talk for a moment about something that at first seemed very incongruous to me, but that I was able to make some sense of as an account of how the God of this world emerges, and experiences its emergence, from the God beyond God.

On page 71, the emergent God says,

> "I am in the midst of Nothing. I don't know who or what I am—I am like a baby in a womb. I hear nothing, see nothing—because there is nothing. I feel alone, very alone, except that I don't yet know what alone means. I feel growing strength, and Myself being drawn toward the light, just a glimmer at the 'edge.' I am in a kind of 'pain,' like stretching aching muscles. Suddenly, it is as if I punch My arms and legs through the sides of a bag I'm in. It is like an explosion. In a split second, fragments are zooming out in all directions."

**Jerry:** That is what, in physics, we call the Big Bang. It is a description very much like those first seconds. Everything explodes into the universe from who-knows-what to the universe as we have it.

**Richard:** When I first read this, I asked myself: How did God get in the midst of nothing? And what is this Nothingness that God is in the midst of? It finally made sense to me when I put it in the context of the God beyond God.

There is a creative process that takes place within the God beyond God, involving a contraction and individuation that allows for the emergence of the God of this world. We can think of this emergence by analogy with a fetus in the womb. At first the embryo is continuous with the mother's body. But at some point, it becomes a distinct individual. Similarly, at first the emergent God is just part of the God beyond God, but then becomes a consciousness, an awareness, unto itself, separate from the God beyond God. And when it first becomes conscious of itself, it is aware of itself as surrounded by a "nothingness"—a something it does not know or understand and feels alone. Aloneness, of course, is the privation of an experience of togetherness. So the experience of aloneness presupposes a prior experience of togetherness.

**Jerry:** Yes. That is why God did not at first feel alone but saw it in retrospect.

**Richard:** God says God felt alone but didn't yet know what 'alone' means. Perhaps to understand what alone means you have to be able to compare it with the feeling of not being alone. Still, this aloneness was a kind of pain, a feeling of privation.

**Jerry:** Yes. It is a privation even though God cannot yet articulate it fully.

**Richard:** This helps answer a question I have pondered in my own reflections about the nature of God, the question of where pain comes from. If you start out with a God who is pure bliss or pure peace, where does pain, suffering, and loneliness come from? How can pain and suffering emerge from bliss?

One way of answering is to say that suffering is a function of the separation that takes place in the creative process itself. As things become separated from one another, individuated, they lose their sense of unity with the eternal and infinite, and this results in an experience of privation, vulnerability, and aloneness that needs to be worked out. They long for the whole, the infinite that they have come to feel separated from. Thus, the emergent God arises out of the God beyond God with a need that becomes a project, which is to work out the terms of this loneliness and longing, which God is only beginning to understand.

**Jerry:** From the very beginning, in that earliest step, the emerging God does not quite know what is going on. Who am I, and what is my function? That emergent God must put order in this flying apart explosion with pieces going in all directions. Meanwhile, God is realizing- I can organize this. My job is somehow to move it in a certain direction, in the direction of integration, though that is still vague to God. These parts are flying in every direction, and God brings them into concert with one another, including God's parts, which needed to be harmonized and brought into functional integrity.

**Richard:** I was very struck, in reading this, by the account of God's loneliness. This is so different from the Western image of God as self-sufficient. Although the notion of God's self-sufficiency raises a problem for Western religion. Why, if God is self-sufficient, should God be so concerned with human beings? What does God want from us? How can God want anything at all from us if God is self-sufficient? But we get an answer to this in your book. God is trying to work something out. There is a project inherent to God's very being, which requires that God involve Godself with human beings. But at first God only vaguely understands this project.

**Jerry:** Yes. God is discovering them as events unfold. In the book, this emergent God is discovering God's role, trying to keep an eye, an orientation toward the telos that is itself a somewhat emerging vision or increasingly definite goal. God is discovering God's self, including God's role, and learns a lot of it, as human beings come into the picture, by interacting with us.

**Richard:** This leads to another interesting point we might make about the emergent God's relationship to the ultimate God. The emergent God is really something of an agent or an arm of the ultimate God.

**Jerry:** It is like an incarnation of the ultimate God. It is the ultimate God for the one world.

**Richard:** Yes, but the ultimate God remains there. It is not as if the ultimate God becomes completely absorbed in its incarnation as the emergent God, and there are other incarnations going on at the same time.

**Jerry:** Yes. That is correct. It is often analogized to an actor. You can imagine an actor in several plays simultaneously. There is the actor going from one part, one role, maybe he is in the same play in two different venues and playing a different character. Yet the kind of placid, rather unchanging God is still back there as the not fully real God because It is not actualized in a world. It is never that the God in this world is less real than the God beyond God. It is more real in the sense that it is actualized in a world. It is like the difference between an architect and somebody who builds a building. The architect has a design but not a building. You have got something actual when you have got a building. So, when God enters the world, God becomes actual.

**Richard:** This leads to another interesting point, which might allow us to reconcile the Western notion of God as self-sufficient with your revelation. The God beyond God needs Its creativity in order to fully actualize Itself, to be sufficient in Itself. If you cut It off from its creative activity, Its need for self-actualization would be unfulfilled. But, in fact, It is *not* cut off from creative activity nor could It be cut off. It is creative by its very nature and there is nothing impeding this. So, perhaps we could say that It *is* self-sufficient, but only *as* a creative force.

This would make it rather unlike Aristotle's unmoved mover, to which everything is attracted, but which has no interest in everything being drawn to it. The God beyond God, on the other hand, is ontologically invested in Its creative activity.

**Jerry:** That is Right. I am not sure I would use the sufficiency/insufficiency dichotomies. Like the composer who writes a score. Why do you actually need an orchestra to play it? The composer, in fact, has the ideal score, the ideal Fifth Symphony, in mind. No orchestra is going to quite live up to the ideal. It is going to have particular players and a particular conductor. Why is it important that we do not just have, instead of the actual played music, a library of scores by the composers? The score, in one sense, is self-sufficient and, if you want to add it, is "at peace." It does everything a score needs to do, but we also yearn for the embodiment of the score in actual performance.

**Richard:** That's an interesting point; the ideal needs to be embodied, actualized, in order to realize what is present in its very ideality. I wonder if we might apply this to the ideal of spiritual peace. In other words, even peace, even the peacefulness of the God beyond God, is not complete until a being who is capable of not being at peace experiences it and finds solace in it.

**Jerry:** Yes. Otherwise, it would be a very inert peacefulness.

**Richard:** In other words, one can only appreciate the peacefulness of the God beyond God when it is contrasted with the disruption to that peace we see in the rest of reality. Looked at this way, this divine peace only really achieves its meaning within the actualized world—it allows us to bear "the whips and scorns of time"—and its true significance cannot be severed from the role it plays within the creation. The peace of the God beyond God—the 'peace that passes all understanding'—would not have the same quality if it were not juxtaposed with the disruption to that peace we see in the temporal world.

This is related to what we called in an earlier dialogue the "integrative" nature of God. In some sense, the whole of reality—the God beyond God, the emergent God, the temporal world, and human beings—are enmeshed in such a way that you cannot fully understand the meaning and nature of any one of them apart from the others.

This integrative nature of God finds very pronounced expression in the relationship between the emergent God and human beings. On page 79, God says,

> **"I could not become a Person without there being other persons. The personal is essentially interpersonal... And so I created mankind."**

This God is developing along with human beings. God only develops in relationship to the development of human beings.

**Jerry:** God develops in relationship with the world, but especially with human beings, because a relationship can be so much fuller with human beings than with anything that has come before them like physical phenomena or animals. Though animals are quite wonderful, God can have a fuller encounter with human beings and learn more from living in their company.

**Richard:** Yes, although the integration between God and humans seems to be even tighter than that between two persons. On page 60, God says,

> **"I am the point of interaction between man and the world."**
> You then ask, "Lord, what do you mean by point of interaction?"
> God responds, **"I am the medium through which man understands the world."**
> And you say, "Is mind the medium?"
> And God answers, **"Yes."**

What God seems to be saying here is that God is immanent within our very consciousness. Of course, this makes God rather different from another person. And there is another place where God says to you, on page 95,

> "I cannot move at a pace greater than the human reactions. That is why it is important for you to tell My story, My history of interactions with humans, from My side. You will see that a development in God is really a response to, (and) conditioned by, the development of human beings and their response to me."

This suggests a very tight integration indeed! Almost an identity. From this vantage point, we might see the religions of the world as explorations of the nature of God on the part of God. In other words, rather than God simply revealing some grand truth to human beings, there is a mutual exploratory process taking place between God and human beings which expresses itself as the religions of the world. God discovers different dimensions of Godself through the emergence of the different religions.

**Jerry:** Yes. That is exactly right and is rather different from a revelational model. In my experience, God speaks to me, and I assume God spoke to Jeremiah, and the Vedic seers, in whatever way God came to them (it may not have been a voice), in a purely revelational, one-direction communication from the Divine to the human. The account in the God book that slowly emerges, as I slowly come to understand it, is familiar with human beings. You and I talk with one another, and our very thoughts come out of that talk. They were not all thoughts we had beforehand. Our personal characteristics start shaping themselves in response to one another. One can become a better person, a worse person, or a more mature person, through the interaction. God is a person, though also much more than a person. God also has cosmic responsibilities, for example. But God is a person in a very vibrant sense, growing and developing in interaction, just as human persons do.

**Richard:** So there is a joint project that both God and human beings are engaged in together, a project of self-discovery and of trying to resolve the negativities of existence. By negativity, we mean pain, suffering, loss, and all the various horrors to which we are subject. These negativities are inherent to the being of the God beyond God and need to be worked through.

In other words, if the God beyond God has a need to create, an impetus to create, because it would go against Its fundamental nature not to create, and if in the course of this creation the negativities of existence inevitably emerge, then this negativity is ontologically unavoidable. And we see this in the book when the emergent God speaks of feelings of loneliness. All of a sudden God has become a separate entity, apart from the God beyond God, and one of the first experiences that results from this is an experience of being alone, no longer fully continuous with the whole. This implies that there is an ontological project implicit in the very nature of being itself, a project of addressing the negativities of existence as best they can be addressed. These negativities *must* be addressed, they cannot simply be wished away because they are inherent to the nature of ultimate reality.

**Jerry:** It might not be correct to retroject all of the negativities into the God beyond God as if that were the sole source of everything. Once you make a world, you have the hard resistance of material reality. The world would not be real unless it were material, and material has limits. Much like the person who has the ideal statue and then tries to put it in marble, the marble has its own resistances and imperfections, and the statue may not come out as perfect as the idea. It would not be right to say the negativity was in Michelangelo; the negativity is in the material.

**Richard:** Right, but in this case, the material itself emerges out of the God beyond God; it is the actualization of something inherent to the God beyond God. It is not like it comes from someplace else. Within the pool of potentialities that is the God beyond God is the potentiality to produce this resistant material. This material is needed for the creation, but also yields negativity. So the negativity is inherent in the materiality that necessarily emerges out of the God beyond God.

**Jerry:** Yes, but God cannot make the material. God cannot make the material out of ideality. The material has to be material. It is in the nature of material. It is not as though God could have made a more perfect material—organisms that were not resistant to age and disease, for example. God does not make up the laws of nature, even. God cannot violate $E = mc^2$.

**Richard:** I agree, but I am trying to draw out the implications of this. The implication is that negativity is intrinsic to the nature of reality, and this presents us with an essential, ontological, project. Everything that emerges is given, so to speak, an assignment, which is to try to resolve as best we can this negativity. This project can be daunting, but also inspiring. It is what allows for greatness. If there was nothing to overcome, what would greatness be?

**Jerry:** It makes for all the positive goods also to be actualized.

**Richard:** In many ways it is a wonderful picture. It provides us a middle ground between Absolutism and Nihilism. Nihilism says that nothing matters, everything is negative, there is no God, there is nobody in charge, and so everything is pointless. The Absolutist says that, if we are going to avoid such nihilism, we must believe in an absolute being who is in control of everything.

**Jerry:** They feed into each other. Each lives off the others' nightmares.

**Richard:** And the book finds a fascinating middle way between these two. The emergent God, even the God beyond God, is not in total control. God is subject to God's own nature. This nature is ultimately good in the sense that, if you can get in touch with it, you would experience that feeling of benign shelter, peace, and love we have spoken about. Nevertheless, out of this nature arises, inevitably, the negativities of existence, which seem to be a function of things separating from one another, itself a function of creation. And this gives us a cosmic, ontological, project—which is to create beauty, to create love, to create peace, to create goodness, out of and in response to the negativity that is nevertheless inevitable. And this project is not only a project to which we have been assigned by God, it is a project God is actively engaged in for God's own self-fulfillment.

**Jerry:** And in which we are co-partner.

**Richard:** Yes, we are co-partners. So this seems to me a very lofty vision.
   I'd like to look at one last passage to sum up what we've been saying thus far. On page 312, God is speaking of the ultimate goal of existence, and God makes it clear that it is not a goal like getting to a finish line. It is an ongoing goal. It is a goal of every moment moving toward its own fulfillment. In a sense, it is the project itself that is the goal.

**Jerry:** That is exactly right. The purpose of a song is not to get to the end. Meaning is in the moments.

**Richard:** Yes, we see an analogy in a football game—the touchdown is for the sake of the game, the game is not for the sake of the touchdown. On page 312, God is talking about the ultimate goal and says,

> "The goal is completeness, connectedness, to create the many and to pull them back into the one."

This sums it all up. We have the Oneness of the God beyond God, out of which continuously flows the Many—many worlds, many things within each world, many gods—and the goal is to bring some sort of oneness, harmony, cohesion to this endless, infinite manyness. And it is a goal that never exhausts itself. You never get to the point where it is all over.

**Jerry:** As you say, the meaning is not in the touchdown; the meaning is not a oneness. It is in the living of the quest for oneness from moment to moment, of living with our lives turned toward the divine—co-partnering minute to minute with the divine in bringing some kind of concert, integration out of the many disparate parts that keep colliding with one another.

**Richard:** I think this is a good place to conclude this session. Next session let's delve more deeply into what we have been calling 'the negative,' that is, the reality of suffering and evil. This, of course, is a major issue within the philosophy of religion, not to mention within many people's lives. Let's see what light the book can shed on this.

**Jerry:** That sounds good. This is a wonderful reading of the book and with many insights that had gone past me. Every text is richer than the so-called author. Here, I am mainly the transcriber. I am sure the book has more in it than any one reader is going to quickly glimpse, including the guy who heard the voice.

**Richard:** Well, that's what we would expect if it is coming from the great beyond!

# 6. The Problem of Evil

**Dr. Jerry L. Martin** You have been thinking, in a very creative way, it strikes me, about how different parts of *God: An Autobiography* fit together. If you look at them in a certain way, you can see them as making a coherent whole and kind of theology of their own. What is our topic for today?

**Dr. Richard Oxenberg** Last time we looked at the big metaphysical picture. We talked about how the God of this world emerges out of the God beyond God and then engages in a great project.
   Today, having laid out that big picture, I thought we might delve more deeply into one of the issues that emerged from it, what is called in the philosophy of religion, 'the problem of evil.' I think your book addresses this problem in a very interesting way.

**Jerry:** It comes up repeatedly in different contexts. It is a problem. We want a solution. There are hints and different perspectives, at different points in the conversation with God, and maybe you see a pattern.

**Richard:** I do see a pattern. So I thought that perhaps we could discuss this pattern and see what you think about it.
   Let's begin, then, by laying out what the problem of evil is, as it is classically understood, and then we'll look at how the book deals

with it. In many ways, religion exists in order to address this problem. Human beings experience suffering and evil and look for help.

**Jerry:** And for meaning- for meaning. What is the meaning of this? Does it mean something? Or does it make life meaningless?

**Richard:** Yes, and we look for it to mean something in order to avoid despair. Kierkegaard speaks of how our experience of suffering and evil can lead to despair.

In Western religion, the problem of evil gives rise to a paradox that, I think, is not very well dealt with in Western religion itself. The paradox might be expressed like this: Human beings face suffering and evil; this is just an empirical fact. As a result, we desire someone, some force, some power, that can help us overcome the suffering and evil we face. Western religion tells us that there is someone it calls 'God,' who is all-good and all-powerful and can therefore save us from suffering and evil. But this leads to a riddle: If God is all-good and all-powerful, why is there suffering and evil in the first place? Why has this all-good and all-powerful God allowed suffering and evil at all?

If we now say that, well, maybe God isn't really all-good and all-powerful, then God no longer seems someone we can rely on to save us from suffering and evil.

So here is the problem: The very suffering and evil that makes us long for God also makes us doubt the existence of God. We are left with this dilemma.

**Jerry:** And a disappointment. And potentially a disillusionment- the despair that Kierkegaard talks about.

**Richard:** Yes, very much so. And it leads, I would say, to a perversion of theology. I am thinking specifically of the Augustinian solution to the problem of evil. Augustine attributes all the suffering and evil in the world to the fact that our first parents—Adam and Eve—sinned.

So it is all our fault. We sinned, and so deserve all the suffering and evil that befalls us. The Augustinian logic goes something like this: God is justly punishing us for our sins, justice is good, and so all the suffering and evil is actually good, it is demanded by justice, which is a good. So it's all good—even though it leads to eternal misery for billions! That's the logic.

**Jerry:** That they deserve it does not seem very plausible. We might deserve a slap on the wrist or on the knuckles, but do we deserve that kind of intense evil and suffering that this world holds? An infant burning in a hotel fire deserves that?

**Richard:** Or eternal damnation, people burning in fire forever.

**Jerry:** There is that aspect. Wouldn't purgatory have been punishment enough?

**Richard:** This theology seems to make God a rather cruel being. This way of resolving the problem ends up not really resolving it at all, because God turns out to be someone we can't really trust.

I think much atheism arises in response to the perversity of this Augustinian theology. The French novelist Stendhal is said to have quipped: "God's only excuse is that he doesn't exist." Many would prefer to believe that there is no God than to believe in such a cruel God.

What I find in your book, however, is a nuanced response to the problem of evil. It allows us to acknowledge the suffering and evil we encounter in the world without either denying the reality of God or turning God into something cruel and evil.

**Jerry:** For openers, the two premises that you cite that we are familiar with in the Western tradition, that God is all-powerful and all-good, are both rejected by God in some of the earliest prayers. I was assuming things and asking now that I have God on the line, is this true or false?

I am given waffly answers that basically say, not all good, not all-powerful. The laws of nature are what they are. God does not make them up or what they are. We work with them in a real world. In ways that are a little harder to understand, God is not all good in the kind of classic sense of eternal perfection.

That does not quite by itself, handle the problem of suffering because, if God has any power at all, God could prevent some of these horrible things. And, if God is not all good, then how is God really God?

**Richard:** Yes, if God is not all good, how can we trust God? And if God is not all-powerful, how is God going to help? One of the ways of addressing this is to modify the claim that God is all-powerful. Process Theology does this. Your work does this as well, and in a rather extraordinary way.

**Jerry:** There is another way in the Western tradition that the problem of evil is handled that is prominent and is addressed in *God: An Autobiography*, and that is that evil is not real. Evil is simply the lack of being.

People like Thomas Aquinas say this in the Western tradition, that evil is simply the absence of good. In the privation theory, evil is unreal. Likewise, there is the Hindu concept of Maya, which takes evil as less than real, similar to an illusion. There is the Buddhist way of saying things, subsistent beings, are themselves unreal. There is a great religious desire to deny the reality of evil.

Against all of those, I am told in *God: An Autobiography*, suffering is really bad. There is no attempt to obscure that fact or say there is a hidden meaning that makes it good or that it can vanish if you think about it the right way- put brackets around it and dismiss it. Evil and suffering is just as bad as those who reject God because of it say it is. So there is a full acknowledgement of the agony. There is full-on acceptance of the agony of suffering and that it is right for us to notice its horrors. In other words, God is not trying to wiggle out of that phenomenological fact, that fact of human experience, that we undergo horrendous suffering. Suffering is really real. And for God too. God suffers when we suffer.

**Richard:** Yes, although it seems to me that even in the context of your book we can understand suffering as a kind of privation, but not in the sense that it is unreal. For instance, we might think of starvation as an experience of privation. The starving person is experiencing the privation of needed food. But, of course, this doesn't mean the suffering is unreal. The suffering is the experience of the absence, the privation, of something we need to be well. So it is privative in that sense, but quite real.

**Jerry:** How do you see the book? How does the big picture surround this issue of suffering?

**Richard:** We talked in the last discussion of the emergence of the God of this world from the God beyond God. The God beyond God is the ultimate reality in the sense of the ontological foundation of all that is, and it is a Unity. There is a place where the God beyond God describes Itself as beyond suffering, beyond evil. There is no suffering in the God beyond God. But the God beyond God, considered in and of Itself, is not complete because the God beyond God has an inherent urge to create.

**Jerry:** There is an ontological difference even there. The God beyond God is like a potential God. In other words, it is quite real, but it is actualized by entering a world and then has work to do. The God beyond God is not fully actualized because it is not embodied. It is like an unborn soul that is floating around, waiting to enter a life and become fully real. In God's unborn state there is total calm, passivity, and peace- a kind of peace of mind.

**Richard:** Yes, a peace. There is an amusing moment in the book where God is saying that the purpose of life is to live it, not for everything to get folded back into the Oneness of the God beyond God. Then you say,

> "So mysticism is precisely wrong, backward."
> And God responds, **"Don't get carried away."**

I love that moment. God is saying that there is a place for the experience of mystical Oneness as well.

But to help us understand how suffering arises from the original peace of the God beyond God, there are two quotes from the book I'd like to focus on. The first is on page 296. God is speaking about the emergence of the gods of the different worlds from the God beyond God, and says that upon first emerging, they 'forget' their connection to the God beyond God.

> God says, **"My self-conscious level (God's Self behind the self) does not forget—though the emergent level (the God of any particular world), in a sense, does (forget). It is as if it is a different personality, beginning anew (in a newly created world)."**

So, in the initial moment of the birth of an emergent god, the birth trauma, so to speak, makes it forget, severs it from its complete awareness of its rootedness in the God beyond God.

This then leads to a quote on page 71. We've looked at this quote before, but I think it is particularly interesting to look at it in the context of our discussion about suffering and evil. God is describing the experience of coming into self-awareness for the first time…

**Jerry:** God and the world are sort-of exploding together. The creation of the world is also the appearance of God.

## THE PROBLEM OF EVIL

**Richard:** God describes the experience this way:

> "I am in the midst of Nothing. I don't know who or what I am—I am like a baby in a womb. I hear nothing, see nothing—because there is nothing. I feel alone, very alone, except that I don't yet know what alone means. I feel growing strength, and Myself being drawn toward the light, just a glimmer at the 'edge.' I am in a kind of 'pain,' like stretching aching muscles."

What is the nature of the Nothing this God experiences, and why does God feel lonely in this Nothing? If we combine this quote with the quote about how the God of this world at first 'forgets' its connection with the God beyond God, we get the image of a God whose being is rooted in something more fundamental than itself, but at first is ignorant of this fundamental rootedness. And this ignorance makes it feel surrounded by Nothing, which is a feeling of great loneliness.

We can relate this to our own experience. The world is made of apparently discrete, independent, separate entities that are all, despite their apparent independence, *inter*dependent on one another. On the one hand, I experience myself as just me. I do not experience myself as the world. And yet my being is dependent on the world. If I were somehow separated from the world I am dependent on, I would experience myself as in the midst of Nothing and very alone. And we feel threatened with the possibility of such separation. We feel this in the dread of death.

It seems to me that it is this threat of Nothingness, and the aloneness that accompanies it, that is at the root of suffering and even evil, at least at the spiritual level. This sense of Nothingness and aloneness needs a resolution.

So it turns out that creation itself gives rise to suffering and evil. On the one hand, creation allows for the great manifold of things to be, to exist, to enjoy existence as distinct individuals. And yet, precisely because the many created things must be separated from the initial Unity that is their ontological base in order to be distinctly themselves, they experience aloneness and the threat of Nothingness. And if you were to feel there to be no way to overcome this aloneness, no way to overcome this entrapment in Nothingness, you would be in despair.

So, we can trace the origin of suffering and evil to the moment of creation itself. It is not anything that God intends, it is a byproduct of creation. And fascinatingly, as the book presents it, it is not only we who are burdened with suffering and evil, while God sits and eats pie-in-the-sky, but God, the God of each world, also undergoes this suffering and aloneness.

**Jerry:** I wonder if this is related to something I was told very early when I objected to why God is so hidden. We are sitting here puzzling, is there a God, is there not a God? You grasp at straws to find evidence. In a moment where I was irritated, God said,

> **"No, I am not hidden, you have to look in the right way."** God still seems pretty hidden.
> 
> I said, "You are sitting up there in divine perfection with the pie in the sky. Why do You even care? Why do You bother with human beings? Why do You want us to do anything? Is human recognition important to You?"
> 
> The answer is yes. **"It is the essence of My being."**

One sees what this means reading through the book, that God is, in God's very essence, related to human beings. God's projects and purposes are, in their essence, related to human beings and to the other elements of creation.

**Richard:** Yes, and this is related to what we have been saying. This God, upon emerging from the God beyond God, is presented with a problem and a project. God must overcome God's aloneness, and God does this through God's creative work with the world and, most particularly, with human beings. So it is not that God is perfect but, for some unfathomable reason, created us with all these troubles. It is a co-partnering, as is often said in the book. God depends on us for God's own well-being in ways that the traditional way of thinking of God would not allow for.

Abraham Heschel has a famous book called *God in Search of Man* that expresses something like this—God needs the human response.

**Jerry:** One needs to add this, I think—there is actual real work in the world to be done. It is not just God needs company or something like that; there is actual work to do in the world. To repair the divisions, flaws, fractures, dividing lines, and tensions, and what the tectonic spheres do when they rub against each other. The world is full of those kinds of earthquakes, and that is essential work. It is not just a made-up project, it is essential work, and God has His role in that and we have ours. We have to be in partnership.

**Richard:** Yes, and this work is a big part of what gives the world its meaning. This is what makes life meaningful. There is something to be done, and it *must* be done. When I say it must be done, I mean that the God beyond God *must* create, the creation *must* produce separation, division, and suffering, and this suffering *must* be addressed. All these 'musts' are intrinsic to reality itself. It is not optional. It is not like it could have been some other way.

**Jerry:** At one point, I thought it sounds almost like video games where you have a character going through obstacles, and each world is like a different video game. Well, no. It is not a video game. This is real. We are real. There is real suffering. There is real good and evil.

You do not really understand the evil unless you fight against it. The evil outside and the evil inside yourself.

**Richard:** Yes, and video games themselves are engaging because they reflect the reality of living.

This then leads to the next thing I thought we'd discuss, related to the quote on page 71, where God speaks of being born. Once again, it sounds like someone coming out of a womb. Let me read the continuation of the passage I read earlier:

> **"Suddenly, it is as if I punch My arms and legs through the sides of a bag I'm in. It is like an explosion. In a split second, fragments are zooming out in all directions. I am at a throbbing, pulsing center. I am not sure what's happening. It is like a tightly coiled spring being suddenly released and springing out into a vast space instantaneously. I scramble to take control, to provide order."**

It is not just God that is being born at this moment. It is the stuff of the universe. And God at this moment is not even clear, it seems, of what God's relationship to all this other stuff is.

**Jerry:** It is the whole of the universe and it is also the Big Bang. God just has the first glimmer that the divine self is supposed to provide some order, that God has a job here.

**Richard:** This reminded me in some ways of Plato's story of the Demiurge.

**Jerry:** In the *Timaeus*.

**Richard:** Yes. Plato's way of dealing with the problem of evil is to say there are eternal Ideas that are perfect but, as in your book, disembodied. Apart from these perfect Ideas is the material realm, which is chaotic. In between the two is the Demiurge, the divine craftsman, who looks up toward the perfect Ideas, then down toward the chaotic material, and tries to order the material in a manner that accords with the perfect Ideas. But because the material is inherently chaotic, the material is always falling away from perfection.

The problem with Plato's scheme is that it makes it sound as if there are three independent things in reality: the Ideas, the Demiurge, and the Material. Plato never explains how these three things emerge or how have they come into relation with one another.

But the book provides an answer. At the foundation of reality is the God beyond God, who is a Unity. Out of this Unity emerges both the God of this world and the matter of this world. The God of this world is somewhat like the Platonic Demiurge in that God has within Godself an intuition of good order—the Platonic Ideas—and struggles to bring the chaotic material that is flying around into conformity with this good order.

God needs to put it into an order that will resolve the loneliness and Nothingness God experiences at the first moment of creation. And this loneliness and Nothingness are resolved through the creation of harmony, beauty, and love.

It is this that gives life—divine *and* human—its telos, its aim. There is a need to create harmony out of the initial chaos, to move toward integration.

**Jerry:** To move it forward to a kind of integration. Exactly. The world is like a diseased body. A person's body is not well functioning when the liver is fighting against the spleen. It is doing some job that it thinks it is supposed to be doing, but in fact, it is spoiling everything because it is not harmonious, not integrated. All of human life, and natural life too, exhibits that lack of integration. God also exhibits this symptom because God, too, is subject to God's own initial limitations. God has to find God's own way.

**Richard:** An interesting quote expressing this is on page 321.

> God says, "**There are forces of integration and forces of disintegration. The latter are sometimes correctly called evil. These aspects of the world are constantly contending, and the world can unravel as easily as progress.**"

We might think of these forces of disintegration as not altogether bad—they are the forces that allow for the diversity of things, for things to be distinctly themselves, separate from the whole. But they can fail to harmonize with one another, which can lead to a state of chaos and even evil.

In response to this mention of integration and disintegration, you ask the God beyond God, "How do You help?" And the God beyond God says,

> "**I am integration, I am ratio, the measure, the order, not just in an ideal sense on paper or on the plane of Platonic Ideas, but I am present in the world, via the empirical God, as its order and integrating telos and motivation.**"

**Jerry:** I am in the world. Right.

**Richard:** The God beyond God is in the world through the empirical God, and the empirical God has the task—not a task God has been assigned, but a task inherent to God's being—of creating order and integration so as to overcome the suffering entailed in dis-integration.

**Jerry:** Let us again make clear, because it is easy to go wayward here and misunderstand the empirical God, the God of this world, the God we encounter, and the God beyond God are not two different beings. The God of this world is simply the God beyond God entering this world and doing His work in this world.

**Richard:** Could we say the same about us and the God of this world—that we are not two different beings?

**Jerry:** I am told we are both same and other. There are presumably good reasons that we are the same. We are a part of the same creation and there is not anything other than God, and we are part of that. At the same time, for us to be partners, for us to relate, for us to love God, and for God to love us, to be in a loving relationship, we have to be different the way two lovers have to be different. They cannot be the same person.

**Richard:** There is something of a parallel between our relationship to the God of this world and the God of this world's relationship to the God beyond God. Does that sound right?

**Jerry:** I have to think that through. There is a little thing with arrows in the book if you recall. The self behind the self is related to God in a way analogous to the way the God of this world is related to the God beyond God. This is not just an analogy, it is also a transitive relation, because my self relates to the self behind the self, which relates to God, which relates to the God beyond God. Implicitly, I am relating to the God beyond God, even if I do not have the concept, because that is the structure that I, and you, and all of us are essential components within.

**Richard:** That is a little hard to wrap your mind around. I have a good friend who talks a lot about the dialectical and paradoxical quality of life. The ontology of life is such that you have to get used to paradox, because you find it all over the place.

**Jerry:** Good point. But you have to be careful in the metaphysical mode not to try to banish all the paradoxes or iron them out, pave over them to make a nice, straight highway. They are there, and the task is to put them in a context in which they mean something.

**Richard:** I suppose we look for a way of thinking about them that will allow both sides of the paradox to be true. The next thing I thought we'd consider is how the forces of disintegration can lead, not only to suffering, but to what we call 'evil.'

On page 53 there is a characterization of what the book calls the 'separatist ego,' meaning that part of us that experiences ourselves as an 'I' in separation from, and even in opposition to, the rest of the world.

**Jerry:** There is in that discussion a distinction between the healthy ego, which is a normal part of a personality structure and helps you cope with the world. Having a sense of yourself, your abilities, your space, and your privacy—that is okay, that is not oppositional. That is just part of your own functional integration.

**Richard:** Again, this is part of the paradox that we always have to remain mindful of. Transcending the ego or overcoming the ego does not mean getting rid of the ego. It means sanctifying the ego. The figure of Christ might be thought of as a revelation of the sanctified ego.

But on page 53, God describes what we are calling the 'separatist ego' in this way:

> **"Ego is destructive, separatist, defiant of My will, self-satisfied and self-lustful."**

This might serve as an explanation for the emergence of evil. The individuated ego, in response to the threat of aloneness and Nothingness it feels due to its very individuation, goes out into the world and tries to control it. It wants to dominate the world it depends upon. Instead of responding to its dependency with humility, it responds with offense: Who are you, it says to the world, to make me dependent? I will make you dependent upon me! And in the course of this, it becomes destructive of others, of other egos. It tries to subordinate all others—really, all other*ness*—to its self-will.

The phrase 'self-lustful' is a wonderfully apt phrase for expressing this because the evil will is, in effect, lusting after its own ontological completeness. It is trying to make itself complete in its very separateness.

**Jerry:** That is a kind of enlarged sense of oneself in a dominion, or a Napoleonic, way. However, we are all interdependent. This enlarged ego insists I will have you all be dependent on me. I will see myself reflected everywhere in the symbols of the empire or whatever it may be. I am the nation. There is no end to that self-lustfulness.

**Richard:** Yes, and there is no end to it precisely because it can never resolve itself. The ego cannot make itself ontologically complete in itself. There is always more that needs to be conquered.

**Jerry:** The world is too big for one thing. Moreover, even if somehow Napoleon did conquer Russia, and went on and conquered China, and ran across the ocean, Napoleon would be surprised to find he is still not satisfied. Still not satisfied because he is still the same crummy little ego that he is in reality.

**Richard:** Exactly. Because no matter how much the ego conquers, it can never make itself its own foundation. It always remains groundless. Martin Heidegger has an interesting term through which he expresses the ego's sense of groundlessness. He speaks of it as a feeling of *unheimlichkeit*, a German word which refers to the feeling of not being at home, literally 'unhomelikeness.' In a sense, when the

God of this world is first created, its experience of Nothingness and loneliness is an experience of *unheimlichkeit*.

**Jerry:** The world is not yet a home. Even though there is a world, it is at its beginning; it is not yet a home. It becomes a home.

**Richard:** Its project—which, as we've said, is also our project—is to make the world a home. There is another passage in the book that expresses this nicely, in the section on Zoroastrianism. God says that evil consists, at least in part, in confusing the good of the part with the good of the whole. The ego is a part, and the ego has a role to play. It is not a bad thing. But if it tries to make itself the whole, then we get into trouble.

We can relate this to the Jewish notion of the *Yetzer Ha-Ra*, and the *Yetzer Ha-Tov*, the evil impulse, and the good impulse. As Judaism speaks of it, the 'evil impulse' is not altogether bad, it is the impulse for self-preservation. But it needs to be subordinated to the good impulse.

**Jerry:** Ambition would be an example. It leads people like Elon Musk to build SpaceX, and to send rockets to the moon. It can lead to achievement. I love a Jewish prayer for God to make good use of your evil impulse too. That is the essence of it. You dedicate your evil impulse as well as your good impulse to God.

**Richard:** In a sense, what Judaism calls 'the evil impulse' is simply the desire to preserve oneself as a separate self, and that is necessary for the creation. Without separate selves there could be nothing but the God beyond God. So separateness is not in itself a bad thing. And the book makes this very clear. This has bearing on some strands of mysticism. There seems to be an idea within certain strands of mysticism that everything would be great if we could just do away with all the egos and have everybody meld into one great Unity.

God says, no, that is not the way, that is not going to get you home. That is not the way to the overcoming of *unheimlichkeit*.

And, at least according to the book, the God of this world, the emergent God, also has something of a *Yetzer-Ha-Ra*—an 'evil impulse'—that has to be disciplined or brought under control. This is discussed in the section on Zoroastrianism, which believed in two gods, a good god and an evil god. And this makes some sense when we think of God as a creature, which the emergent God is. The God of this world is a creature, a very sublime creature, but nevertheless a creature. The God of this world is not the ultimate ontological ground, except in so far as God is connected to that ground.

**Jerry:** I have never thought of that; that is the lack of integration. People need to pay special attention to the chapter on Zoroastrianism because, for historical reasons, the religion did not last. Zoroastrianism was a major religion, the religion of the Persian Empire. In the Old Testament, God speaks of "my friend Cyrus," who is a Zoroastrian. But then Alexander the Great marched across Persia and dismantled the traditional religion, and then much later, Islam marched through in an iconoclastic way and destroyed their texts. The priestly types who knew them by heart reconstructed the text. It is a religion that has had a terrible fate in the history of the world and has been retrenched in a rather narrow way. However, I consider it one of the major revelations.

**Richard:** Zoroastrianism serves as a kind of segue from polytheism to monotheism. It is on the way to ethical monotheism. The way it is presented in the book, the two gods of Zoroastrianism—the good god and the evil god—are two aspects of the one God of this world.

**Jerry:** One aspect is the resistant side of God.

**Richard:** On page 177 God says,

> "Just as your desires or temperament sometimes seem to have a life of their own, so some of My aspects have a life of their own. Among the things I must order and provide direction to are My own aspects. I do this through Wisdom, My own calm center that purviews (views or oversees) all, assesses all, weighs it in the balance, placates (pacifies) disturbances."

He relates this to the struggle between the two gods of Zoroastrianism:

> "This was really Me, struggling to supersede other aspects of Myself."

**Jerry:** This is part of the story of the development of God. Zoroastrian revelations and divine interaction with Zoroaster himself is all part of the story of God's efforts toward greater integration and of God's self-reflection on what that is like. He does this by putting it into a kind of drama as if there were two different Gods- a good one and an evil one. It is really the one God struggling for mastery over God's self.

**Richard:** So there is within the emergent God something of an egoistic temptation that God has to address and overcome. And this might account for some of the ways God may not have responded to human beings in the most optimal manner in the early days.

**Jerry:** God said- I was young then. I had to learn. That was the first time I got a glimmer of God as a developing God. That made no sense to me at the time. God was young in this world and, like any of us, has a biography. Well, that is why God gave me the title of the book, *God: An Autobiography*. These are elements of God's biography and Zoroaster charts the central dynamics of that story, or it is charted in the revelations he received.

**Richard:** There is a way in which this God, as an individual, is going through, at a mega level, something of the same maturation process that we human beings have to go through. And, indeed, there is a tight integration between these two maturational processes. God's progress depends upon human progress. God says that in a number of places.

**Jerry:** Yes, God does. That is because God is a Person. Like all of us, you do not become mature by sitting alone and thinking about it. You become mature through interaction with other people, your parents, your family, your coworkers, your friends, and you discover aspects of yourself and learn from your mistakes. The key to life is good judgment, and judgment comes from experience, and experience comes from making mistakes. God goes through that with human beings and that is God's biography, and we are an essential part of that story, just as parents and siblings are the central part of the younger person growing up.

**Richard:** All of this helps us better understand the project that God is engaged in, a project of creating harmony, which is to say, relations of love. It is really a project of bringing all the disparate elements of the creation into a relation of love.
A quote on page 111 expresses this nicely. God says,

> **"You see My drawing the physical world toward life, and drawing life upward to greater possibilities of love; to creating man (and) drawing him (people) into loving relationships with his (their) fellow creatures, with nature, and with Me."**

A world in which such love would be actualized would be what Jesus calls "the Kingdom of Heaven," a world in which we love our neighbors as ourselves, love nature, and are in loving relationship with God. This would resolve the *unheimlichkeit*—the sense of Nothingness and aloneness—that God first experiences upon emerging into the world.

Another fascinating quote, also from page 111, helps us put all this into perspective. God says,

> **"Remember that love is what fully actualizes a thing. A person comes into full personhood only in a loving relationship, in loving and being loved."**

What struck me in thinking about this quote is that the God beyond God, although not suffering and experiencing evil, nevertheless has a longing, a longing for actualization. That is why the God beyond God is not sufficient unto Itself. It needs to create this problematic world and turn it into a world of love. Only thereby are the potentialities of the God beyond God fully actualized. And there are an infinite number of ways in which this love can express itself, in all the many worlds. This, then, seems to be the fundamental project that each of the worlds, in their diverse ways, are engaged in.

In this context, we might look at one last quote, from page 347.

> **"The ultimate triumph over evil and incompleteness is to be in tune with the God inside you and to express that divine love to others."**

So, the way to finally overcome the potentiality for evil within us is for the ego to enter into communion with the love of God, and then to share this love with others. This is the solution to the problem of evil. And we have no choice but to struggle to resolve this problem. There is no opting out. It is a project inherent to the very nature of reality, a project toward love that must be accomplished. And this gives life great meaning.

And the book also tells us that there is great hope. On some level, we are told—some supra-temporal level—this project is already complete, and we can take solace in that, though this doesn't mean we can lay back and do nothing.

**Jerry:** No, it has to be accomplished in time, in the temporal dimension within which human action takes place. But there is another perspective from which, like opening a novel in which events happened in a certain sequence, you can open it at any page and you can see them from a point of view outside the temporal sequence. There is nothing to see unless they actually happen and happen in time. Nevertheless, you can open the book at any point, even skipping to the happy ending if you want, and see it happening.

**Richard:** This allows us profound hope. We will not finally be left in the *unheimlichkeit,* the Nothingness and aloneness. Salvation is inevitable. We can rejoice in that. But still, we have to do the work.

**Jerry:** One has to do one's part in one's own lifespan. There is this other point of view where one is not stuck in one's own moment in time, but can open to any page and take it in. This offers a hope. It is a deeper understanding or higher understanding—a more adequate understanding.

**Richard:** Yes. We are told that we can get in touch, even now, with this consummate moment. This reminds me of the famous psalm, "Though I walk through the valley of the shadow of death…"

**Jerry:** Of the shadow of death, yes.

**Richard:** "…I shall fear no evil, for thou art with me." There is some sense in which we can, even now, be in touch with the ultimate moment of resolution.

**Jerry:** Yes. What is later called the Victory Level.

**Richard:** So, to sum up, the book provides a resolution to many of the paradoxes and problems surrounding what theology calls, 'the problem of evil.' There is a reason why there must be suffering and evil, and we cannot simply dismiss them. They are not an illusion. But not only are things not hopeless, there is a path toward their resolution, a resolution in beauty and love that we will all inevitably take. Still, we have to work at it. And this very fact makes life deeply meaningful.

**Jerry:** It is in the Victory Level not just at the end of time. It is not just about what will happen a million years from now. From another perspective, that is already real. We can relate to it. We can connect with that ultimate victory in some way that is not filled out in detail.

**Richard:** Yes, and this is why we should not entirely dismiss the mystical. In some ways, the mystic is the one who is trying to have an experience of that Victory Level even in the present moment.

Maybe we can close this discussion here. Next time I thought we would focus on the book's account of the human being. Thus far, we have been focused on the nature of God and revelation, but the book has a lot to say about the nature of human beings as well. So perhaps we can focus on that in our next talk.

**Jerry:** This is wonderful work you are doing, Richard, and I just hope the readers find it as fascinating as I do because it is very impressive how you fold these parts together.

**Richard:** Thank you, Jerry.

# 7. Nature of Human Beings

**Dr. Jerry L. Martin** Where do we start today's dialogue, Richard?

**Dr. Richard Oxenberg** Hi Jerry. In the last few sessions, we've talked about the nature of God. Today I thought we'd focus on the nature of human beings and human life as presented in the book. The book is very geocentric in many ways, focused on the earth. It speaks, of course, of other worlds, but not of other galaxies and planets within our own world.

**Jerry:** The other worlds are more something like other universes.

**Richard:** Yes, and the book paints a broad evolutionary picture, similar to Darwinian evolution, except with a teleological dimension not present in classical Darwinian theory.

**Jerry:** It is evolution as development through time, but not in the sense of Darwin's explanations for it, which are entirely mechanical and due to random factors. There is a direction to it, which there was not for Darwin. For Darwin, it is all chance and natural selection. It is just a fact that some things survive and some do not. So, on that view, nature is not trying to get somewhere. By contrast, there is a sense of right direction present in *God: An Autobiography*.

**Richard:** The direction is toward an expansion of consciousness, starting with primitive modes of awareness at the vegetative level and moving forward to higher and higher levels of consciousness. And we are told that this evolutionary process is continuing and will continue beyond human beings as we know them. God says,

> **"Remember that I am learning all the way. I do not know what the final product may be. Man, as he now exists, is not the final product—only the future will tell us, including Me, that."**

**Jerry:** Yes, God does not know.

**Richard:** God does not know, or at least did not know. If we think about the simultaneity of time discussed later in the book, there is some sense in which God would or could know, but the book tells us that God's consciousness is also in the process of developing. This might allow us to reconcile God's statements that God knows there will be a final 'victory' with this statement that God does not know what the future will bring. Might it be that, given God's development, God did not know in the past but does now?

**Jerry:** Well, I did not ask that question. There is great stress, in fact, on unpredictability, both because of elements of free will, freedom on God's side and our side, and maybe elements of unpredictability, the way everything is unpredictable. God blocks my temptation to say that God now knows the future by saying I am confusing the flow of time, within which the concept of "now" makes sense, with a non-temporal perspective in which there is no "now."

And then there is the creative element. That may have some sense of direction, but the sense of direction always seems to be inside emergent possibilities rather than a pre-planned destination and route for getting there.

**Richard:** Yes, there is a general sense that there are higher possibilities to be attained, and that there is a general thrust toward these higher possibilities. At one point, talking about the evolution of consciousness, God says,

> **"Consciousness developed very slowly. . . . Whitehead and Teilhard are on the right track in this regard. Leibniz is not."**

What do you take that to mean?

**Jerry:** Well, Whitehead and Teilhard have a sense of creative possibility and of nature moving forward in a direction. Speaking of emergent possibilities sounds very much like Whitehead. Teilhard, a paleontologist and evolutionist, has a somewhat different sense. Teilhard was a student of the stages of life and saw life advancing toward a much higher stage of consciousness, which he outlines in his writings. Leibniz conceives of multiple possible worlds. Our world is constituted by how it unfolds in each individual consciousness, each one mirroring the whole. Of all the possible worlds, this is the best one already. There is no dynamic development in Leibniz.

**Richard:** Another thinker we might throw into the mix here is Sri Aurobindo, the Hindu-Indian thinker. He also has a sense of life developing in an evolutionary process toward higher and higher levels of consciousness.

**Jerry:** Aurobindo, perhaps the greatest thinker from the Hindu tradition of the last hundred years, is quoted in the book.

**Richard:** Certainly one of the greatest. So, the universe is evolving, and God is also evolving. Let's look at a quote on page 82. God is describing Godself at the time of the earliest humans. God says,

> "I do not quite know I have a personality, an individual personhood. Events pass through My consciousness."

It is almost as if God has not fully awoken at this point. God says,

> "I have a sense of My intelligence pervading the world, of fulfilling a universal telos. I feel a spiritual rapport with life. But none of that constitutes a sense of personhood, of an I standing opposite a You."

God only learns of God's self as a person in the context of being in relationship with human persons.

**Jerry:** Exactly. You can only get a sense of yourself as an I in relation to a You if there is a You to encounter and to relate to. It is not unlike accounts of neonate consciousness. At first, there is just a world, and the neonate, mother, and everything surrounding is just one flow of consciousness. Only slowly does the little baby realize this is me, and that is mom, and these are physical objects, this is my body, and it is different from the chair. All of that evolves.

God is at this early stage. Think what that would be. God is born. God has burst into being (in that creation section) with the universe and is part and parcel of the universe. It is all just happening. God does have that early sense that God has to put order into this universe and move it in a direction, but that is all just happening. There, as yet, is no sense of a personality. The concept of personality would not even have a role yet, since the concept of a self implies another self. That happens a little bit with animals, but they are so limited that it only happens in a fuller way once there are human beings, like the prehistoric humans.

**Richard:** So, God goes through a long gestation period. If we think of the Big Bang as having happened 14 billion years ago and the emergence of human life as happening only a million years ago, there is a pretty long process here before God fully comes into God's own as a person—close to 14 billion years.

**Jerry:** Long by our measures. We do not know what that would feel like to God. God is not marking time, not bored the way we might be, but, yes, for many years, God is just busy with the physical universe.

**Richard:** And this is related to an idea that pervades the book—quite different from the way we ordinarily think of God in the Western tradition—of God's interdependency with human beings, although the word 'interdependency' almost seems an understatement. There is an intimacy between God and human beings that seems almost symbiotic. God says in a number of places that God develops *through* human beings.

On page 95, for instance, God says,

> "I cannot move at a pace greater than the human reactions. That is why it is important for you to tell My story, My history of interactions with humans, from My side. You will see that a development in God is really a response to, and conditioned by, the development of human beings and their response to me."

In this quote it almost sounds as if human beings have the initiative; God is developing in *response* to human beings. Or at least it is a tightly integrated relationship.

**Jerry:** It could be that they are simultaneous, like two people who, left alone on a desert island, suddenly meet one another. Then they will start being defined as social beings by that encounter and, in fact, develop social capacities and realize aspects of themselves that they did not realize before, such as how they react to someone else staring at them, smiling, or shaking their hand. They start learning not only about the other but also about themselves. They learn what it is to be a person in the social mode, which on a desert island, they had no opportunity even to think about before.

**Richard:** Here's another quote along these lines on page 103, God says,

> **"I understand My nature better as I articulate it or as humans hear it, process it, and articulate it."**

I am struck by the fact that God's self-understanding and the human understanding of God seem to coincide. Almost as if God's mind is somehow within the human mind.

**Jerry:** Let us go back to our two guys on the desert island. If I say something and you laugh, I suddenly realize I am funny. I did not know I was funny before. I may not have even had the concept of being funny. The laughter shows another aspect of me in our interaction. So we are expanding ourselves precisely by learning about ourselves and how others respond to us.

Once again, that parallels the literature on babies and childhood. How does a child learn about love? Well, it is from the mother's love. We all learn these things through interacting with other people. God is in the same mode. God is developing and learning from us, which is a lot of the point of the book.

God told me to read the ancient scriptures of different religious traditions. Well, what are those scriptures? They are narratives of people reacting to God or the divine as they are experiencing it, thinking about it, writing about it, and articulating it, often in prayers and songs of praise.

**Richard:** It is almost as if a process of individuation and differentiation is taking place over the course of Cosmic evolution. Originally, there is no clear differentiation between God and everything else, there is no clear sense of I-ness within God. Looking at the quote on page 82 again, God says,

> "At this point I do not quite know I have a personality, an individual personhood. . . The protohumans gave Me that, or I developed it or became aware of it in relation to them."

Human beings develop in such a way as to require a God, and God develops in response to the human requirement for a God. There is a teleological, evolutionary, process behind this that neither the human being nor God is responsible for initiating. They are both a product of the process, not the initiators.

The process itself is emerging from the God beyond God; that is the initial impulse and the basis of the teleological process. It is only at a certain point that the emergent God becomes a truly self-conscious entity and then tries to figure out the divine role in relation to human beings.

An example of this is on page 326, in a discussion about the development of Hinduism. God says that God discovers the Atman in the course of human beings discovering the Atman:

> "From India, I learned another side of Myself. Long before Lao-Tzu had written about the inner attitude to the Tao, the seers who wrote the Upanishads had made a major discovery. They had succeeded in contacting Me through their inner selves. They had discovered the Self behind the self, and they had discovered—and I discovered, when they connected with Me in this way—that the Self behind the self, which they called the

> Atman, is Me, which they called the Brahman. 'The Atman is the Brahman.' This was a revolutionary step in the human understanding of the divine reality, and it was a critical evolutionary step in My self-understanding."

Once again, human beings are discovering God *for* God. It is a process of self-discovery taking place simultaneously and interdependently on both the human side and God's side.

**Jerry:** In a very early experience before I thought about the Atman or any such thing, God tells me to blank out the outer world. Suspend awareness of it. I knew how to do that. You draw into your own states of consciousness. You have your internal moods and bodily sensations; you become more acutely aware, from the inside, of where your arms are and the weight of your body on the chair beneath you.

Then I was told to blank out and suspend my own flow of consciousness as well. I did not quite know what God meant, but I gave it a try. That is when I had this sense of the Self behind the experienced self—the self behind the empirical flow of consciousness and embodied consciousness. A further dimension of self is observed. It is like the ordinary sense of self, but has rather different characteristics of stillness and dispassion, yet is benign and interested, but not interested in a sense that causes it to be striving. That was my toehold on understanding the Atman when we come to the Hindu context.

The Self behind the self that I was experiencing unites with what the Hindus call Brahman, the more fundamental reality, and what we might call God or a divine presence.

Back to the part you are highlighting, Richard. God says it was through the human discovery of the Self behind the self and the human perception that the Self behind the self is identical to (in some sense) the divine or some aspect of the divine. That is another way God discovers and relates to people, actually as a part or an aspect of people. This is different from saying we are all part of creation, that God and we are all part of the God-world that comes into being at the creation. There is this further intimate connection through the Self behind the self that is virtually, without pushing concepts of identity, it is virtually an identity, or type of fundamental connection.

**Richard:** Do you still feel connected to that level, Jerry?

**Jerry:** Yes. I describe that experience, which I had early when Abigail and I were on vacation, to an extent. I have never asked a Hindu to certify it as the Atman, but it is my avenue into understanding the Atman. I felt the Self behind the self. It did not occur to me at all that it also connects to the divine. I had to read about the Hindu scriptures before that thought came to mind. I had mystical moments not long thereafter, but they did not directly connect to this experience of the Self behind the self.

**Richard:** Can we think of the individual Atman as a conduit between the human individual and God?

**Jerry:** It is one conduit. In my dialogues God makes it quite clear that this is not the only way of connecting with God. Hindus may think it is the primary way, but there are several ways, each of which has its own virtues and dimensions as an intimate self-to-self connection with the divine. The Atman of God is just one way I found it natural, or found it coming through to me, to think of the God beyond God. The way it came through to me does not seem to be the same as is articulated in any particular religious tradition.

**Richard:** Yes, although I'm not so much thinking of a way of connecting with God, which we can do through prayer and ritual, etc., but I'm thinking more ontologically. The Atman is represented in the book as the ontological bridge between the individual and the divine.

There's a diagram on page 309 that shows this through a series of arrows linking God to the human being through the Atman:

"**Atman of God → God → Atman of man → man.**"

The diagram implies that God is connected to the person through the Atman of the person.

**Jerry:** The Atman of God is one way I conceptualized the God beyond God. But, since there are many bridges, I hesitate to draw the ontological conclusion you are drawing. I do not have anything against it. If that is how it works, that is fine. It would be a beautiful explanation.

**Richard:** Let us talk a bit about the Atman of human beings. Unlike the Hindu conception, the book tells us that even the Atman is undergoing a process of development.

**Jerry:** It did strike me, as I learned more about Hinduism, that my concept of the Atman in these dialogues with God is that Jerry has an Atman, and Richard has an Atman, and both our Atmans are, within the Hindu frame, identical with the more fundamental reality, Brahman. Hindus might already find the Atman to be non-personal. It is already the pool of the divine that we are diving into, in other words. You are going on to the further thought: Does the Atman itself then develop and not just ourselves in the personality sense, but the Self behind the self? Does it also undergo an evolution?

**Richard:** It would almost have to given that God is developing and the Atman has its basis within God. The only thing that does not develop is the God beyond God, but the God beyond God is invested in the development of everything else.

**Jerry:** That, you might say, is its development—though your statement, Richard, is more precise. It is really that the God beyond God has a benign interest in the God of each particular world and in the people of each world.

**Richard:** We have yet to mention reincarnation and the notion that the individual human life does not terminate in death. This is relevant to the question of whether and in what way the Atman develops. According to the book, human beings have been involved in this world since the beginning and will continue to reincarnate.

**Jerry:** Early in the book, I share the three different visions of the afterlife that I received, which resembled my thinking before my dialogues with God. The afterlife is something like heaven, some special state, better than the life we now know.

A further dream I noted, but did not initially explore, was after a brief time in heaven, where I saw loved ones again and had a loving view of the whole world, I saw what appeared to be myself being born in a basket in a rice paddy in China. I thought that was strange. So, there had been a time in a heaven-like state and then a rebirth into the world. I did not like reincarnation, so I only prayed about it later.

**Richard:** So, there are different stages in the afterlife. There is something similar to a heaven experience and then a reincarnation into corporeal life. So this raises the question: How are we developing through these different incarnations? Are we now more complete in some sense because we went through all these incarnations?

As the book presents it, it is the Atman that is learning and growing through these incarnations. We see this on page 230. You say to God,

> "So it's not that Jerry Martin now knows more than his earlier incarnation but less than a later one. It is

that the Atman, which is continuous across lives (and perhaps even outside our time system), is learning." And then God says, "**Yes, that's correct.**"

If we put this together with our earlier discussion of the way God's development is linked to human development, we get a picture of God learning through the Atman of human beings, and the Atman of human beings learning through the individual lives of human beings. The individual lives of human beings are not themselves progressing—although in some sense they must be if they are expressions of the progressing Atman.

**Jerry:** Thinking of the Hindu conception, I asked many times whether the following is how it works: do well in this life and come back at a higher status, do poorly and come back at a lower status.

The view of those multiple lives that reincarnation implies and that I received in my dialogues with God is that the point of each life is not going up or down. The next life is not a reward or punishment for however you lived in this life. If you live badly, that is, you might say, permanently on your record, but you come back to experience something new and to have a new set of challenges.

It is more like you have written a symphony; now, write an opera. Or, you have been a policeman, now be a crook, that is, now have the challenges of someone born in a high crime environment, like some of the characters in Charles Dickens's novels. Each life has its challenges, and the purpose is to meet those. By implication, the Atman, the Self behind the self, is enduring and would be accruing these experiences, insights, and spiritual development. It is much as we go through a single life now and have multiple careers, relationships, and interests. We try this and that, like one kind of music now and another kind of music later. We go through many different things, from each of which we learn something, and we become richer, deeper, more complex selves as a result. With reincarnation, we do that same sort of thing through multiple lives.

## NATURE OF HUMAN BEINGS

**Richard:** You ask God about karma—or actually, God *tells* you to ask about karma—on page 226.

> God says, "**Now, ask about karma.**"

**Jerry:** Yes! Occasionally, God tells me what to ask. If I ask something, God may say that it is the wrong question or ask about something else instead.

**Richard:** You say, "Now I understand karma as less a matter of making up for past wrongs and more a matter of which challenges a person needs next."

> God responds, "**No, that is not right! Karma is a matter of 'righting the balance' after the imbalances of your previous life. Remember how I have told you: Don't feel guilt, just note the consequences.**" And then God goes on to say, "**Life is for a purpose and the purpose is not just entertainment. It is to achieve a result.**"

Then you say, "To achieve balance?"

> God says, "**That's okay for now. When you achieve balance, there is no reason to be born again.**" (Although this seems a little inconsistent with the discussion about reincarnation).

Then you say, "Then spiritual liberation *is* the goal?"

> And God says, "**No, balance is. 'Liberation'—misnamed—is the result. It is a karmic consequence of a life 'balanced out.'**"

What exactly does this mean? What is balance?

**Jerry:** That is an intriguing question in light of what God says about different challenges, but I did not go back and pray about it more. It suggests that if you went off the deep end in one life in this way, the next life, it is unclear what balance would mean—go off the other deep end? You would need a sense of range, which makes sense for many of life's tasks. Say, you have written many poems using the standard definition of sonnets, rhymes, and meter patterns. Now drop all that and do something completely different. Do a free verse. You will expand your understanding. It could mean that you need to stop being so extreme or need at least some lives where you are not extreme. Not extreme does not necessarily mean balanced in some perfect sense, but at least living life modestly, moderately, or something commonsensical. What did it suggest to you, Richard?

**Richard:** I had some difficulty understanding this, but it began to make sense to me as I thought about the association God makes between balance and liberation. God says that when you achieve balance, that is liberation.

We might connect this to the book's presentation of reality as an interrelational system. On the one hand, every individual has to be themselves as an individual; there is something sacrosanct about our individuality. But, on the other hand, we also have to exist in a harmonious relation with the whole. So to live well we must find the right balance between self-involvement and other-involvement, a balance necessary for the health of both. In other words, for our self-involvement to be healthy it must be balanced by a healthy other-involvement, and vice-versa.

A wonderful image of balance is the Buddha sitting on the lotus flower. On the one hand, he is perfectly contained in himself, and, on the other, he is in relation to everything around him.

This need for balance can be related to what we spoke of in an earlier dialogue concerning the danger of chaos inherent in the individuation process. As each thing becomes distinctly itself, it must separate from everything else, but then, because reality is a whole, each distinct thing must enter into harmonious relation with the whole to be well.

**Jerry:** God gives me a musical analogy. The meaning of Beethoven's Fifth Symphony is not the final notes but the whole thing. It is a complex score with many things happening and many different kinds of instruments doing their different jobs. The meaning is in the whole thing; it is not the final moments. The final moments just have to be congruent with the whole thing. They cannot somehow displace it or distort it.

Our lives in the world have that element of complexity that we bring. Think of those opening scenes of the creation chapter when the whole world is exploding in all directions, and God has to arrange order. So, part of the picture is always a high degree of complexity and multiplicity. The word harmony is often used, which you have just cited, Richard. They all need to be in harmony, which does not mean boiling down to one thing as though you made them all into a thin soup or reduction.

**Richard:** The image that is coming to me now is of wholes within wholes. Systems within systems. To continue with the musical analogy, for any individual musician in the orchestra to play their particular instrument well, they have to make all the notes they are personally playing work together. They have to balance all those notes. So, there is a particular role for each to play individually. Then there is a role that all the musicians have to play together, and it is only insofar as each plays his or her part right that the entire orchestra will be able to play that particular movement in the symphony right. But that movement must exist in right relation with the other movements in order for the symphony as a whole to achieve its telos or goal. And the symphony as a whole is itself part of something grander and greater than that.

**Jerry:** It is just one symphony in a whole world of music, and music is just one part of a culture and one part of a given life. Even Beethoven's life had parts other than music- other loves and losses. You are right, Richard. It is wholes within wholes within wholes all the way up.

**Richard:** This may be where the idea of balance comes in. The parts of each whole must be balanced in relation to the other parts in order for them to work together as a whole. And each whole must be balanced with the other wholes in order for the 'whole of wholes,' so to speak, to achieve its telos. And once you've achieved that, it's not like you then say we can go home now, we're done. That is when you can first experience the beauty of life to the fullest. So it is toward such balance that everything is headed. And there is no point at which this process ends. It just keeps getting richer and richer.

Perhaps we might think of the difficulties we face in our individual lives as challenges that demand of us that we find the balanced way to address them. As we find that balanced way, our Atman grows and we are able to more fully experience the beauty of life.

**Jerry:** Right. There is always more to be done. I always thought the afterlife sounded boring. God told me, "No. Let Me give you another way of seeing the afterlife." Imagine the most beautiful music, more beautiful than any actual music has ever been, the most beautiful scenes even more beautiful, and you are more able and have a greater capacity to take them in. The greatest love and being loved, and the greatest intellectual "aha" moments with deep, fantastic insights. Well, all of that, you can certainly call joy; you can call it many things, but it is very rich, noble, rewarding, and fully actualized.

**Richard:** Each incarnation has the potential to move us forward, every life has a truth that we need to find. On page 232, God says,

> "Every role or life task-challenge-mission has a truth and has a falsity, in the sense of limitations… just as each work of music or poetry or each athletic event has its own mission, obstacles, keys to success, tendencies to failure, to overreaching or underachieving, facing or failing to face the truth of that mission. Succeed or fail, one learns something, and the universe learns something."

So each individual person comes into the world with their own particular project or duty—their own dharma. It reminds me of the Bhagavad Gita, where Krishna says to Arjuna that he must fulfill his dharma.

**Jerry:** Duty in the ultimate sense.

**Richard:** If we put this together with our discussion of the Atman, we arrive at the idea that it is through each individual life pursuing its dharma that the Atman is able to grow and learn and achieve greater wholeness. So we each have a calling, and an urge to satisfy that calling. And, of course, given the immensity of reality, there can be, even must be, many different callings.

**Jerry:** The calling need not be noble, like saving the world. It can be the calling of coping with the miserable difficulties in your situation, coping with a disability or having an alcoholic mother. All kinds of things are included in the truth of our lives. In this situation, I have these capacities. I do not have other capacities that I wish I had; I have just these. Our first task is understanding that and taking in the truth about ourselves. There is not just one mission for each life, though maybe it is correct to say there is a central mission. Every day has its own callings as well. Those are important to pay attention to, as well as the larger sense of life projects or missions.

**Richard:** Finally, let us say something about where it is all heading. The title to section 65 of the book reads: "The victory is now and the struggle is now." What do you understand that to mean?

**Jerry:** Well, it is a very important line, and it is in the final part of the book called Victory, sometimes referred to as the Victory Level. We are in this world, and we must face its challenges, including coping with the evil outside and inside us. So we are engaged in that good fight all the time if we are doing our duty, and at the same time, even though we may be losing that day or even lose in some large way, the victory is now. We are fighting to achieve victory with daily ups and downs. There is another perspective from which the victory is already achieved. Part of that is connected with the fact that, as I am often told, time is not what we think of it as being. There are some analogies given at different places in the book. I never probed that very much; it always sounded too abstruse and theoretical, but I was given some analogies to help me make sense of it. There is a perspective from which you can see all different times, and the victory is present from that perspective. It is not that the victory occurs at the end of time, but it is right now. Right now—as seen from a different point of view. But "right now" does not mean the same as "now" as marked in the passage of time. It is "now" at a level "outside" the temporal sequence. But we can relate to that Victory Level, as it is sometimes called.

**Richard:** So there is one sense in which we are moving toward an endpoint. But in another sense, and perhaps even the more important sense, the purpose of the endpoint is to enrich our lives now. And one of the ways it enriches our life now is by giving us the peace of knowing that the endpoint is there. I am reminded of the revelation bequeathed to Julian of Norwich: "All will be well, and all will be well, and all manner of thing will be well." Knowing this provides us a great sense of peace in the now.

I will read a last quote from page 342. God says,

> "The fulfillment just *is* the drawing upward."

So fulfillment is not in resting at the top, but in being aware of the top as we strive to make our way toward it. Every moment within life has the potential for awareness of this Victory Level, and to be aware of the Victory Level as we engage in the struggle for victory *is* the fulfillment.

> God says, "There is not some perfect moment hidden there that makes it all okay. The symphony of everything reaching up toward My glowing presence *is* the fulfillment, the triumph over evil, over negativity, over the void."

So, every individual reaching up toward the whole while remaining an individual is the fulfillment of its individuality.

**Jerry:** The victory or fulfillment is in reaching for the divine, and the whole provides the context. In a sense, it is simple. Our job each day, at each moment, is to live Godward. Live our lives in and, you might say, for God, and from God, to the extent we can.

Our lives are mainly full of practicalities and setbacks, and we stub our toes. One understands that, but to live one's life where one understands it all in this transcendent, upward attention toward the divine, with that sense of purpose of working in harmony with the divine, is victory. The meaning of my life is not in the stubbed toe. It is in my Godward attention, sometimes called the Victory Level.

**Richard:** And the possibility of stubbing our toe, the potentiality of the negative, is inherent to the nature of being. It is something we must struggle with. There is no escaping this; there is no other place for us to be or other reality we can move to. But the negativity cannot and does not supersede the positive, and we must grow to realize that.

**Jerry:** Yes, that is right. Negativity does not define our lives unless we let it. Even if we let it, we will get to a place where we will realize that it is not the defining reality. We should not let it define our lives. There is a viewpoint from which it does not win.

**Richard:** Maybe next time we can start to look at the different religions as you were directed to examine them in the light of this new revelation. I thought we might first have a discussion about the Western religions, then a discussion of the Eastern religions, and then a discussion in which we reflect on the relationship between the two.

**Jerry:** Having your insightful, careful reading of *God: An Autobiography* is wonderful, Richard.

**Richard:** Well, thank you, Jerry. Very good talking to you as always.

# 8. World Religions

**Dr. Jerry L. Martin** What is our topic today, Richard?

**Dr. Richard Oxenberg** Today is our day for looking at the Western religions. The God of the book says that God underlies all the world religious traditions. This, of course, is rather different from the schismatic way the religions tend to present themselves. But we are told that this is not the proper way to look at religion. We are told that all the different religions are different aspects of one fundamental truth, despite the fact that they often say different things.

**Jerry:** They do, in fact, say different things. They are just different aspects of the divine revealed in those traditions.

**Richard:** What I thought we'd do for the next three sessions is focus first on the Western religions, then on the Eastern religions, and then have a session in which we talk about how West and East might be related to one another.

**Jerry:** The big, big picture.

**Richard:** So, let's begin. We've talked about how God emerges out of the God beyond God, creates human beings, and then tries to establish a relationship with them. Out of this relationship emerge the different religions. The religions reflect the human experience of being in some relationship with God. This experience finds expression in a wide variety of religious forms throughout human history, and there does not seem to be a culture (except perhaps in the very recent period) that does not exhibit some sense of being in relation with the divine. Looking at a quote on page 139, God says,

> **"One reason I'm telling my story now is that today it is time for mankind to begin to sort out what is true and not so true in the various religions and other sources of insight and to piece them together into something more adequate."**

**Jerry:** Yes. This is a project that could not have been done much before our own time because now the religions are all so much more aware of one another and have many communications—such as inter-religious dialogue—that are not hostile. And, also, as scholars from multiple cultures study one another's traditions, they come to appreciate them. At first, I wondered why *God: An Autobiography* was right now. That was because I had not paid attention to what was going on in religion. As soon as I looked around the world, I saw that this is the revelation for our time, for the 21st century, that could not have been earlier. It would not have made sense. God could have said it, but it would not have made sense to anybody. Now it does make sense.

**Richard:** Yes, I think it makes a lot of sense—the basic idea being that there is a truth to the idea of God, a truth to the idea of the divine, but it is a grand truth that can't easily be reduced to simple terms. And rather than see the differences of the various religions as opposed to one another, we should see them as expressing different dimensions of that grand truth.

God says on page 90, "**I came to all peoples, but arrived in different guises. I came to the American Indians as the Great Spirit, to the Moslems as Allah, and so on. I came to the Hindus in many forms, and hence their many stories.**"

At one point, you ask why God didn't simply tell everyone the whole truth from the start.

**Jerry:** Yes. Why dribble it out as the Great Spirit to the Plains Indians, as Krishna, and as different forms to other people? Why not just give the whole shebang to people, one big story? What you have quoted I often quote in talks. It is a very important passage.

**Richard:** God responds, on page 101,

> "**Your question has presuppositions—that I have given different incompatible stories to different cultures. This is only apparently true. If you think them through, they are different pieces of the same puzzle.**"

In other words, the human apprehension of the divine is like a grand puzzle with many different pieces; if we can figure out how the pieces fit together, we can begin to approach the ultimate truth. In this context, you began a project called Theology Without Walls.

**Jerry:** It is late in the book, in fact toward the very end. God gave me the assignment of starting a project that would start to put the pieces together- Theology Without Walls. Theology has always been done in a very narrow way. They call it confessional theology, where each person does the theology of his or her own religion, or denomination. Lutherans do Lutheran theology and so on. If theology is to be the articulate understanding of the divine reality, then that is way too narrow. It is not the understanding of the Lutheran divine reality but an understanding of the divine reality that all of us on the planet Earth live under. We all live under the dome of heaven. We live under the same divine reality. So let us start studying that. It was a challenging task for me because I, first of all, was a philosopher, not a theologian. Only recently having an interest in religion, I knew nobody in the world of the American Association of Religion- a very big organization of theologians and religious studies scholars. I started attending and getting to know people, and then finally, God said it was time to launch the project, and it has been very well received.

**Richard:** Yes. And it was in this context that you and I met.

**Jerry:** You were at that first meeting in San Diego. We had a planning meeting, and people showed up whom I had not met before, and you were one of those. We met at the original planning meeting after we had done one panel at AAR.

**Richard:** Actually, I think I first met you at a second meeting in Atlanta, but it doesn't really matter.

One question that comes up, of course, is why it was necessary for God to give different pieces of the puzzle to different people rather than just give everybody the whole picture at once. We get an answer on page 139. God says,

> "The total revelation would be more than any single individual or culture could bear or well act on. So there is a kind of division of labor. For example, I told the ancient people of Israel to act in history and to keep My covenant and abide by a set of religious and moral rules. That was task enough for them. I told the ancient people of India to develop the inner life and to get in touch with

> the transcendental Atman, the Self beyond the Self. Both were and remain valid tasks."

**Jerry:** That makes sense. Imagine saying: Here are the Ten Commandments—and also meditate and go through this challenging process that Hindus go through contacting the ultimate Brahman. It would have been absurd. It was hard enough to give people the Ten Commandments and get a Covenant going. You can say the same for these various other religions. In fact, each one has a very spiritually full plate.

**Richard:** Yes. And it fits well within the evolutionary schema that we have been discussing. Until recently, human beings weren't sufficiently united and advanced to be able to take in the whole picture. If God is now asking us to piece it all together, this suggests that we have arrived at a new evolutionary stage. We have finally arrived, after a long difficult development, at a point where we are able to look upon the whole as a whole.

**Jerry:** Yes, that makes sense, and that is what has happened. People had religions at odds with one another up until about 300 years ago. They were killing each other to save each other's souls. That does not make sense, right? These are Christians killing each other, and that does not seem very Christian. Is this what Jesus taught? No.

We had to go through those stages of development in different cultures for them to have their own stories and evolutions. And we had to get to that point of developing an interest in one another, a lower level of hostility, and greater levels of mutual understanding. As a result, as I was told at the end of the book, we stand on the threshold of "a new axial age"—a movement toward more profound understanding and spiritual transformation.

**Richard:** In recent years, we've had a number of thinkers—Wilfred Cantwell Smith and John Hick come to mind—who have developed the idea that we have arrived at a time in history where the religions can begin, not only to tolerate one another, not only to respect one another, but to be fertilized by one another.

**Jerry:** Exactly right. A lot of it is from post-World War Two. Aldous Huxley wrote a book, *The Perennial Philosophy*, in 1947. One avenue is to think, as he did, that all the religions say the same thing. You might say they do it at a certain level if you abstract it a bit. For example, none of them are materialistic and greedy. They all have a kind of mystical level. And he emphasized the mystical as the level he preferred, but there were other religions that do not quite say the same thing. But they can all be different stories of one thing. They can be understood as pointing to the same thing but not as saying the same thing.

**Richard:** One of the Perennialists whom I've found interesting is Frithjof Schuon, who distinguishes between what he calls the 'esoteric' and the 'exoteric' level of religion. At the exoteric level, religions say quite different things, but those exoteric differences are inspired by the same esoteric truth.

**Jerry:** The exoteric tends to be the popular religion. Every religion often contains all kinds of little superstitions, all kinds of overly concrete ideas about the divine. The esoteric were considered more mystical and spiritual experts- people who developed the spiritual life to the highest level and therefore did not need these excessively concrete views of popular religion. That was one very sophisticated form of Perennialism.

**Richard:** This is related to a basic theme that runs throughout your book, the paradox of the relationship between the one and the many. There is one ultimate truth, but that ultimate truth, by its very nature, manifests itself in an almost infinite variety of ways. Therefore, human culture, reflecting this, also manifests itself in a great variety of ways. And, given this, it would be almost impossible for all human beings to have the same exoteric religious practices, because those practices have to align with the specific cultures, and those cultures are different.

**Jerry:** There are really two reasons the religions are different. One is the cultural diversity. Like artists, cultures are working with different palettes, different sets of colors, and color instruments. Those are the cultural frameworks people are working with. The other reason is God then coming into the culture and working with that, "Oh, these people are very good at watercolor, so I am going to do watercolors with them." In fact, in doing that, God then actualizes, manifests, and develops an aspect of the divine reality. It is a fulfillment being expressed in a certain tradition, in a certain way. God gave the people of Israel the Ten Commandments and the Covenant. God gave the people of India the task of connecting with the inner dimensions and to the divine via the Atman, the Self beyond the self. God thereby was using the situation and cultural talents of the people of Israel and of India.

**Richard:** Yes, and a complicating factor in this whole story is that God is developing God's own self-awareness as human beings are developing their awareness of God. So God really couldn't have given everyone the whole picture at once because God is discovering the whole picture *through* the human discovery of God. There is a co-evolutionary process going on.

**Jerry:** Yes. One sees in the Bible the development of God as a lawgiver. One of God's basic jobs in the world was to establish norms. God does this in different ways with different cultures. Only one culture got the Ten Commandments, for example. So others can build on that. God is discovering the divine capacity as a lawgiver. In famous passages like Sodom and Gomorrah, when Abraham argues with God, part of the argument is to remember your role.

Abraham is saying to God that one of the implications of being the lawgiver is that you have to abide by reasonable rules yourself. You have to provide justice. Just wiping out a whole city because of the sins of a few is not justice. So we see that evolution of God, in that tradition, in that way, and you have similar developments in other traditions of God discovering aspects of the divine self, and those becoming developed in the back and forth with human beings. That continues today.

**Richard:** Yes, this can be a little difficult to wrap one's mind around if one comes at it from a traditional understanding of religion: God is discovering God's nature *through* the human discovery of God's nature. It is not as if there is a complete, fully known, truth to which each culture is responding differently. The process of human's discovering God is part of what allows God to discover God.

**Jerry:** Yes. The divine reality will respond as we respond. The divine reality will also actualize Itself more fully in our response.

**Richard:** There is a codependency.

**Jerry:** I do not like that term.

**Richard:** I don't mean it in a pathological sense.

**Jerry:** God and ourselves work with one another and can only work with one another. Both divine and human actualize ourselves through that interaction.

**Richard:** There is an interesting passage on page 45 that speaks to this. God says,

> **"The old religions were mostly based on insights, revelations I gave them. But they became rigidified.**

> **Partial insights were mistaken for the whole. Ritualism and creeds have been overemphasized, and I am Myself partly to blame, since at one point those were the most important things in the world to me.**

God says on several occasions about this period, "well, I was young then," which is, once again, strange when we think of it in traditional terms. But it makes sense if we understand God to be developing God's self-awareness through the creature's awareness of God.

**Jerry:** Yes, it is so strange. Yet, like any two people, the personal is interpersonal.

**Richard:** It might now be helpful to walk through the book's presentation of the way the awareness of God develops in the Western religions. We start out with paganism, a polytheistic view, then we move toward a dualistic view with Zoroastrianism, and finally, to monotheism, the notion that God is One. All of these different ways of looking at God have validity.

**Jerry:** Yes. They also express genuine signs of the divine reality. Polytheism expresses something genuine about divine reality. It was not the final and complete story. Because it is not, the story moves on.

**Richard:** God says on page 92, speaking about polytheism,

> **"Any religion that does not allow for this aspect of My presence—My presence to nature, in objects, in places, and in forces—is missing something."**

**Jerry:** Yes. The point of polytheism is not the Greek pantheon we think of with Zeus and Hera. It is more of the way people regarded special places as sacred, and forces of nature as sacred. The lightning or the storm was expressing the divine, and sacred mountains and rivers. And sacred moments, the moment of death, for example. These are all distinct moments, God says, you cannot talk about it generically. Not every storm is a divine message, but those are among the ways God communicates. The world is like a finger painting, and this is like God's signature painting and one way of coming to us. If you leave that out entirely, as the purest kind of high theology might tend to do, then you are missing something. What you are missing is God's presence in the world.

**Richard:** This gives some validity or sanction to the Neo-Pagan movements we now see emerging in our culture. People want to get back to an appreciation for the sacredness of nature. Some criticize Western religion's insistence on the transcendence of God as having the effect of desacralizing nature. We have come to regard nature as merely a thing, a repository of resources, rather than as an expression of the divine.

**Jerry:** Yes, merely as something to be exploited. It is important to keep these dimensions in our conception of the divine and not overly purify the concept. Otherwise, we end up with some abstraction as our concept of the divine and as our only way of relating.

**Richard:** So, then we move into Zoroastrianism. We talked about this a couple of sessions ago with respect to the question of evil, but we can look at it again in the context of the development of religion.

**Jerry:** These are powerful revelations. I believe Zoroastrianism was a major world religion and should be in textbooks covering the nine major religions. It was historically unlucky because Alexander the Great marched through, and then some centuries later, Islam marched through with anti-iconic tendencies. There were a few huddled Zoroastrians who went to India and became a very self-referential group in order to survive. If you read the texts, these original revelations—which we believe we have, even though the documents were destroyed, because the priests had memorized them. We probably have something very close to the actual words of Zoroaster himself as he reports the revelatory experiences he had. It is a dramatic picture.

**Richard:** That's interesting. I have never personally read Zoroaster. I always thought of Zoroastrianism as a kind of stepping stone between the polytheistic religions, where nature is full of different gods, and monotheism—although maybe that is not the right way to look at it. There is an interesting dialectical play between monotheism and Zoroastrianism. On the one hand, a problem with monotheism is that if you attribute everything to one God, it is hard to account for evil.

**Jerry:** Yes! If there is one powerful God, everything that is bad in the world is all laid at that God's doorstep.

**Richard:** Yes, but on the other hand, a problem with Zoroastrianism is that if you envision reality as a battle between two equally powerful forces opposed to one another, you do away with the idea of reality as a unified whole.

**Jerry:** Zoroaster saw that in the world was a second deity who sometimes appeared to be the other half of the major God. That is the side described as his twin, as though this might be the other side of God. This twin, called the Hostile Spirit, is going to inevitably rise up and try to contest God's dominion in the world. He is going to contest the good, just because it is good, and turn people against God. The story of history from then on is the story of the struggle. Somehow, from the beginning, God knows good is going to win, but the Hostile Spirit does not know that. Even if he knew he was going to lose, he would still fight because of his meanness and wickedness. He cannot help himself; you might say, that is who he is. So you have this contention that goes on, and at one point, the people who live in a kind of slightly unreal, ideal world are given a choice. Do you want to stay up here in this ideal but not quite real realm? Or do you want to come into the world and help Me fight the Hostile Spirit? They all volunteer to go to enter the world and join the fight.

**Richard:** What the God of the book tells you is that *both* of these spirits are dimensions of the one God. On page 325, God says,

> "I am not all-good—or, as he [Zoroaster] put it, there are two gods, one good and one evil, contending with each other. I am not exactly contending against My evil side, but I am incomplete, and I am running up against My limitations and that sometimes leads to perverse consequences."

**Jerry:** Yes. God says explicitly in certain exchanges that it is mainly God's lack of integration, as if it is an organic metaphor. What is the problem when we get sick? One part of the body often does not co-operate with the other parts. It is producing too much of something or not enough of something. Somebody once asked if cancer cells are ugly under a microscope. A medical scientist said, "No, they are actually quite beautiful." They are not unhealthy in themselves. In fact, they are too robustly healthy, so they start taking over. So it is as if God's problem is that in this long course of evolution, God is slowly learning to integrate different aspects. The world is very complex, the divine reality is very complex, and the tasks in view are very complex. Just as we cannot command our bodies to stop our liver from malfunctioning, God cannot instantly tell some aspect of God's self to stop.

**Richard:** I've often thought that at the core of evil is the desire of the part to take over the whole.

**Jerry:** That fits the organic medical analogy perfectly.

**Richard:** The part comes to see itself as ontologically threatened precisely because it *is* a part and not in command of that on which it depends. Out of this sense of being threatened, it tries to take over the whole it depends upon. And this leads to what we call evil. The part seeks to dominate, to subject, and to destroy whatever it can't dominate. We might think of envy and resentment, as well as greed and concupiscence, as rooted in this drive.

The spiritual response to this, which we see in Christianity and other religions, is to get the part to recognize its need to harmonize with the whole. The part must come to see that its true happiness and security will come from communion with the whole rather than from conquest of it.

**Jerry:** Right. That is a good analysis.

**Richard:** And this struggle between that within us that seeks communion with the whole and that within us that seeks conquest—which in some sense is the battle between good and evil—finds expression in Zoroastrianism. And this struggle is still going on in the world today, and within ourselves. We are still engaged in this battle. So, there is legitimacy to this Zoroastrian way of looking at life.

**Jerry:** Yes. The battle is internal and external, moral and spiritual, and it goes on all the time, which is, in a way, what the story of life is, and what it is all about. It is not pointless. It is not meaningless. It is not purposeless. It is replete with purpose. It is an ongoing struggle to achieve integration, harmony, and full-relatedness.

**Richard:** It is in this context that monotheism becomes necessary. In order for there to be a possibility of integration, harmony, and full-relatedness there needs to be a whole the parts can harmonize with. If we represent reality as two contending parts, each trying to destroy the other, then there are just two evil forces.

**Jerry:** Well, no, not both evil. One is good, but they are just two parts.

**Richard:** But what makes one good, if each wants to destroy the other? If each wants to destroy the other for its own sake, how are they in any way different?

**Jerry:** Well, the true God is not just trying to do it for God's own sake but for what is good and noble and beautiful in the world, for what is right.

**Richard:** Yes, but what is good and noble and beautiful is harmonization with the whole. That's what makes the good and evil spirit different from one another. The evil part wants to conquer everything, and the good wants to commune with everything, including, I would imagine, the evil part. The desire of the good is not to destroy the evil but to convert it or somehow redeem it.

**Jerry:** Or to make use of it for the greater harmony.

**Richard:** What is producing all this discord and evil is itself part of the whole. So the next revelation needed is the monotheistic revelation that there *is* a whole, a whole that includes the evil part. In a sense, you have to rise above the dualistic Zoroastrian vision to a monotheistic vision in order to make sense of the distinction between good and evil at the heart of the Zoroastrian vision. We might almost say that monotheism is already implicit in Zoroastrianism.

**Jerry:** You are making sense, but you are going rather beyond the book. I ask late in the book, is monotheism the story? I am told no. It is just part of the story. Zoroastrianism is still part of the story. Polytheism is still part of the story, as other religions that are not theistic. The personal aspect is just one aspect of the divine reality. So do not think we are all headed toward monotheism, the summit and culmination. You talk about the whole. Monotheism is a part that wants to be the whole, but there is a larger whole. The key is that the whole has to be extremely complex. Philosophizing and theologizing tend to simplify or boil everything down to one principle or ultimate reality and eliminate that complexity. One of the main things we learned from *God: An Autobiography* is how complex the divine and the world are—how manifold the tasks are and the kinds of life to live are. Consequently, each one is actualizing yet another good. Harmony is not one thing where we end up with a single note going on forever, but it will always be a very complex, dynamic harmony.

**Richard:** Yes, it is somewhat paradoxical, isn't it? A proper appreciation for the whole requires an appreciation for the great diversity making up the whole. Still, it does seem to me that the book lays out something of an ultimate goal—which is for the part to enter into communion with the whole while retaining its distinction as a part. In one way or another, all the religions are moving toward this. And if we think of evil as the part trying to take over the whole, then this ultimate goal is the overcoming of evil as well.

**Jerry:** That is a possible formulation.

**Richard:** Let's now move on to the book's treatment of the God of Israel. God says, on page 90,

> "The God of Israel is one face of Me. It is really Me, and I really did undergo the development recorded pretty accurately in the Hebrew Bible."

Here you discuss with God some of the specific events recorded in the Bible, like the creation of Adam and Eve. I stumbled over this a bit because it seemed to contradict the book's evolutionary picture. God speaks on page 86 and 87 of first creating Adam and then creating Eve in response to Adam being alone. This, of course, is right out of Genesis. But how do we reconcile this with the evolutionary idea that human beings evolved from the great apes, which the book also says?

**Jerry:** I do not take that Adam and Eve part to describe the history and development of our human biology or evolution. I consider it a kind of myth. God explains to me its meaning. God was alone. As you say, God was lonely and, in some sense, created human beings in evolutionary history. God can now become a fuller person in an interpersonal relation. Eve is created so that Adam can become a fuller person in an interpersonal relation. The problem is that it is somewhat diagnostic. There is not much evolution within this story or development. One would have to come back and think about that.

I take it to describe the timeless human problem. God created this wonderful world, using that creation language, and gave us all these wonderful capacities of enjoyment. For example, sexuality and creativity. Having gotten them, we tend to think they are ours. It is much like what you were saying about nature. We treat it as a resource for us. Similarly, our bodies become instruments of our own pleasure, and our capacities in the world become ways to dominate others. Why not climb to the top of the corporate ladder or become the richest person in Idaho? All these talents and good things we are given in the world around us become completely detached from God's purposes and from our partnership with the divine. It is as if Zoroastrians, people who have signed up to come to the world to help conquer evil, once they got to the world, relax and say, hey, this is great, let's live it up! That is what I take God's comments about Adam and Eve to mean.

**Richard:** So, you don't see this as God speaking of something that actually happened in history but as God providing an interpretation of this mythological story?

**Jerry:** Yes, that's right. It is one way God captures essential truths. The expulsion from the Garden of Eden is not so much a literal story of being expelled and punished—detachment from God *is* the punishment. We are told in various places, you are not punished for your sins, your sins punish you. You become a crummy person because of your sins. That is an affliction. You might not know it, but that is an affliction.

**Richard:** That is helpful. I have always taken these stories as mythological and it was not clear to me, reading the book, that God is also saying they are to be read this way.

**Jerry:** Well, it would depend on the story. You cannot just say it is all a myth. This is the myth of Adam and Eve. A character like Abraham is often called legendary, not just mythological. He is not a kind of made-up character to be an allegory or something of the sort. When I prayed about whether this really happened, God said not to worry about that; something like that happened. There was somebody who first heard God's voice. Later, you move into historical time. People like Jeremiah, the prophets, David, and so forth are of historical times, and there are records. The records do not always match the biblical account, but they do show that something like that was going on, in fact.

**Richard:** As the book lays it out, all of this development—from Adam through Abraham through David, etc.—culminates with Jesus.

**Jerry:** Just be careful. It is not culminating in the sense of replacement theology or that we leave the people of Israel behind now and move on. It is just another stage when we get to Jesus. The original Covenant is still valid, but Jesus comes along and does what Jesus does.

**Richard:** Yes, it is not supersessionism. Jesus adds a new dimension but doesn't negate the Jewish approach to God. But let's talk a bit about the significance of Jesus, as the book presents it. On page 17, you say, "Lord, is Jesus Your Son?"

**Jerry:** Yes. I asked all these standard Christian questions because I grew up in a Christian home and a Christian culture. I ran through a whole list of standard Christian attributes and ideas, including whether Jesus was the "son" of God, and what that means. Does that mean he is sort of God?

**Richard:** In response God says,

> "**Yes.**"

And then you say, "Lord, is Jesus God?"
> God says, "**Yes.**"

And then you say, "But you told me I should not become a Christian."

At one point you asked God whether you should become a Christian and God said no, is that right?

**Jerry:** Yes. At one point, I thought maybe I was supposed to be Jewish, and I did not look forward to circumcision. Then I was told- no, do not become Jewish. And then I thought, should I become Christian? I was told- no, it is a sect.

**Richard:** Yes. God says,

> **"To believe that Jesus is My Son is not the same as being a Christian. Christianity is a sect, with some truths but many limitations. Study Jesus, learn from him, but do not become a Christian."**

Now that, of course, is a message specifically for you. God is not saying that nobody should be a Christian.

**Jerry:** That is right. For the purposes of this project, God may have just had a sense for me not to be affiliated because I am going to read the sacred texts of many religions and ask what God is doing with each one. Perhaps it was best that I do not have a dog in that fight. That might be the reason. At one point, I started to say something about the Trinity, and God just said, do not go there. We are not doing Christian theology, in other words.

**Richard:** Historically, the book never goes past Jesus. You do not go into the development of religion after that.

**Jerry:** God said to pray about Jesus going into Jerusalem, not Jesus coming out. I took that as a cut-off period for all the religions and prayed about the ancient scriptures, the revelations, and in the case of Jesus, what he was saying, and what he was teaching in the Gospels. Do not go off into Christianity and doctrines, do not go off into Buddhism and the many sects and philosophical developments that Hinduism also has. Do not go into the religions; just read the revelations. They are ancient. So, these are the ancient revelations cut off at roughly the time of Jesus' life.

**Richard:** There is a poignant moment in which you ask God whether the Jewish people should have accepted Jesus as Messiah, and God says yes. You talk about how Abigail, your wife who is Jewish, reacted to this. You said she cried.

**Jerry:** She held back when I had these experiences, as she explained later when I asked why she did not say anything. She took it all in. That was clear because she remembered what I had been told. She said she thought it was a delicate thing I was going through. She did not want to create static. On this occasion, I was told the Jews should have accepted Jesus as their Messiah. She told me later when I inquired (only when I inquired) that she had gone off and cried. She cried because she was so aware of the enormous price Jews paid at Christian hands over the next thousand-plus years up until very recent times, and all unnecessary. I guess that was what was striking her, that all this suffering was unnecessary.

**Richard:** Of course, it's relevant that, as the book itself points out, Jesus and Christianity are two different things. Very few Jews had a direct encounter with Jesus during his lifetime. So what the Jews rejected was the way Christianity presented Jesus to them, which they believed violated what they had been told from God.

**Jerry:** Yes. Jesus was saying uncomfortable things, and the strict Pharisees would argue that he was wayward. Christians forget that Jesus was not a Christian. Jesus was a Jew. Everything he said he was saying to other Jews, presumably made sense to them, was understood in their familiar terms. Subsequently, for a time, what we now call Christians were a sect of the Jews—the Jews who followed Jesus. There were various sects and strands within Judaism, and the followers of Jesus were one of them. Later, as Christianity grew in power, the two became more hostile to one another and more competitive. Part of the scriptural text reflects that the gospels were written several decades after the life of Jesus and usually not by first-hand witnesses. Scholars differ about that. There ended up being this terrible competition, and the Romans at first persecuted the Jews and the Christians—they were lumped together in their minds. Then Christians ended up with imperial power and, from then on, Jews became targets of Christian persecution.

**Richard:** And the way Jesus is presented in the book is not exactly Christian orthodoxy, right?

**Jerry:** At this point, I was not putting questions of Christian orthodoxy forward for a yes or no from Jesus. I was just having a dialogue about what was on my mind when I first encountered Jesus while reading some of the New Testament and asking Jesus about events depicted in the Book of Mark.

**Richard:** I'm thinking of the fact that, though God says that Jesus was God, God also says, on page 196,

> **"All people are, in a sense, God made flesh."**

So, Jesus is not metaphysically unique. God is not of a different substance than human beings, as is believed in classical Christian orthodoxy.

**Jerry:** Yes. That is very striking. Jesus is also unique. Not unique in contradiction to what you just quoted, Richard, but Jesus has a role that you and I do not have. Jesus has a cosmic impact.

God is not so transcendent. Christian orthodoxy goes back to God as Creator—taking that first line of Genesis to heart, and maybe reifying it somewhat or freezing it in place as a doctrine. If God is going to be the Creator *ex nihilo*, then God has to be completely different from the world God creates, as the potter is different from the pot. More puzzling, if Jesus is going to be God, you must have some strange incarnation of God somehow coming into the pot, into this totally created material world. In *God: An Autobiography*, God and the world come into being together. They are aspects of the same spirit, and we are aspects of that spirit, too. Therefore, that is part of why our communion with the divine is possible. We do not have to leap out of the world in order to connect with the divine. The divine is here in us, and Christians have known this in spite of the creation doctrines. Augustine talks about God being "closer to me, than I am to myself." Christians often affirm that God is literally everywhere.

**Richard:** On page 248, God says about Jesus,

**"He is the pure embodiment of love."**

That's what makes him unique. All human beings are 'God made flesh' in some sense, but he is unique in being more fully infused with divine love than the average person.

**Jerry:** Yes. Jesus is 100% divine-filled. We are different. We are all God in some ultimate metaphysical sense, but in terms of spiritual actualization, most of us are various percentage points far below 100%.

**Richard:** You ask about the traditional Christian teaching that Jesus died as payment for our sins. On page 286, in a dialogue with Jesus himself, Jesus says,

> **"That doesn't even make sense. Sins are not debts to be 'paid.' They are a condition to be healed, rectified. The solution is not for me or someone else to suffer or sacrifice or otherwise 'pay' for them or 'redeem them.' It is for each person to become more perfectly attuned to Me."**

That also gives us a rather different understanding of the role of Jesus than we get from traditional Christian theology.

**Jerry:** I know of a very strongly believing Christian who is also not a very good guy. He is a rather sharp dealer, a cuts-the-ethical-corners realtor. He always talks, with glee, about how Christ saved the Old

Testament David. David was a murderer and womanizer, and so he thinks, "I have not done anything as bad as David." Christ is the get-out-of-jail-free card in that theory. The *God: An Autobiography* view is: No; the solution—salvation, if you use that term—is a closer spiritual attunement to the divine. That is salvation.

**Richard:** So the significance of Jesus is to reveal to us someone who has arrived at that sanctified state, which helps us, through devotion, contemplation, and reflection on the spirit of Jesus, to move in that direction ourselves.

**Jerry:** Yes, because God seems very distant to people. I heard this voice, so that is not my personal reality or situation. On the whole, God seems very, very distant. Whereas Jesus lived, he is a historical figure. We can imagine what he looked like, and we know the stories of what he did, many of which are well-verified through historical sources. Historians have verified more about the life of Jesus than about Alexander the Great, who is a more distant past figure. We do not challenge that. Well, we know a lot about Jesus, so we can relate to Jesus. From my experience of Jesus appearing to me, I have had the feeling afterwards of Jesus almost physically being in my heart, of having Jesus inside as a friend. God says Jesus is more available, but you do not have to go through him to get to God. I mainly talk to God even after I encountered Jesus. But if you do relate to Jesus, it is transitive—relating to Jesus relates to God, and so 100% of you can relate to Jesus in that way. It goes right through to the total divine reality. That is the picture.

**Richard:** Perhaps we can wrap this session up with some discussion of the book's understanding of the kingdom of God. You ask God about the line in the Gospels in which Jesus says, "there are some standing here who won't taste of death until they see the Kingdom of God."

**Jerry:** I challenged that; it seemed like a bait and switch to me.

**Richard:** God responds, on page 278,

> **"The Kingdom of God is the reception into the soul of God's presence. It occurs to people during this lifetime, not afterwards and not at the end of history. They, those select individuals to whom he [Jesus] was speaking, understood this. A crucial part of this communication is that I am using Jesus both as the messenger—he is an Elijah—and (as) an exemplar—he is God. He is God, and I am saying through him that they *can* be 'God' and that he *is* God, and by participating in him, they can participate in Me."**

**Jerry:** That is the Kingdom of God. To have that kind of relationship with the divine, which Jesus, in a very special way, makes possible for people. That is salvation, the real story, and, in some sense, the meaning of history. What is the meaning of the world? Why is there a world? What is the drama of the world? It is to move toward that kind of relationship with the divine, which you can do right now, though it is hard. You do not wait around for it. It is not the afterlife. There is an afterlife, but the real action is here. Although, as we discussed, there is also a point of view from which time transcends just calendar and clock time, and it is a kind of eternal truth. That concept is this higher point of view that is not trapped in our linear time. From that point of view, you are already there. You have arrived at the kingdom of God, and it has been realized.

**Richard:** And to arrive at that state would be the overcoming of evil, at least within oneself.

**Jerry:** Yes, that is a good connection- within one's own self. The greater half of the struggle is internal. How do you live your own life, which is internal, in external relations? You have to be ethical. You have to treat others properly, or you will not be tuned in properly. You will have cramped your spiritual capacity if you treat others badly. The solution is the spiritual connection with the divine that, living rightly, you can achieve with an open heart.

**Richard:** So, today we have discussed the Western trajectory of religion. The book also goes into the Eastern trajectory of religion. One of the things the book calls on us to do, at this moment in history, is to see how the two fit together. Next session, we'll talk about the book's treatment of Eastern religion.

**Jerry:** Very good. Perfect. Perfect.

# 9. Eastern Religions

**Dr. Jerry L. Martin** Well, Richard, what is our topic for today?

**Dr. Richard Oxenberg** Last time, we looked at Western religions. Today is our day for looking at the Eastern religions. I've been thinking of that famous line of Rudyard Kipling, "East is East and West is West, and never the twain—"

**Jerry:** "And never the twain shall meet." But, they did meet. They certainly meet in this book.

**Richard:** Yes, so today we'll focus on how the book treats the Eastern religions, and next session we'll talk about how to put it all together. One principal difference between the Western and Eastern religions is the way they envision God. The Western religions tend to represent God as a person, something like a human person 'writ large.' But there are problems with understanding God on the model of a human person. One of the main ones, perhaps, is that human persons as we know them, are exterior to one another.

**Jerry:** Yes. Good point.

**Richard:** God, on the other hand, is supposed to be on both sides of the I-Thou divide. I think one of the reasons Eastern religions have gained popularity in the West is because the Western representation of God as a distinct person creates a sense of distance from God, and also allows God to seem threatening. If we are part of God, as the Eastern religions tend to say, God will not want to hurt us. If God is a distinct person, as the Western religions tend to say, God could theoretically be as hostile to us as other hostile people are.

**Jerry:** God can even smash us. Especially if God also sets rules and norms and is a kind of judge. Which is, you might say, one of God's jobs—to establish norms within each culture. That can be threatening- you will get rapped on the knuckles if you do something wrong.

**Richard:** You may get a lot more than a rap on the knuckles. You may get thrown into hell for all eternity! That idea is rejected in your book; God says there is no eternal hell.

**Jerry:** The whole goal of God is saving all of us. According to certain theologies and sects, even after you go to hell, you can work and get back out again. You can work your way out or have grace reach down and save you. That is the problem with hell. We might do a whole session on the implications for human living because these things about sin and hell are very important to how we should live.

**Richard:** One of the ways your book gets beyond some of the problems associated with the personhood of God is to suggest that God is a very *unusual* person. God can be experienced or related to as a person, but we should not think of that as the ultimate metaphysical reality of God. On page 243, for instance, God says to you,

> **"You relate to me personally, and see other revelations as glosses on that experience. But they could just as well see your relation to a personal God as a gloss on Brahman or Buddha or the Tao."**

This reminds me of the paradox between waves and particles we see in quantum physics. Sometimes photons appear as waves. Sometimes they appear as particles. And this suggests that their actual reality is neither a wave nor a particle. They are something more fundamental that can manifest itself in these different ways. Something similar seems to be true of God. God is not a person as we ordinarily think of a person, but nor is God a mere impersonal force as we ordinarily think of an impersonal force. God is something beyond both of these and can manifest in both a personal and transpersonal manner.

**Jerry:** That would be one interpretation, just as that is one interpretation, but not the only one, of quantum phenomena. I take it that God is the divine reality that *has* these characteristics. In other words, it is not some other who-knows-what that manifests or becomes one thing, and then becomes another. The divine reality is very complex and has multiple aspects, some of which are personal, and some are, in various ways, non-personal or transpersonal. In the Eastern religions, we see that they have become aware of the transpersonal or less personal. Each is a separate story, even though one can generalize about the Eastern religions. They are picking up other aspects of the divine, thereby helping to actualize those aspects. Even though they are not interacting with God as a person or the divine in a personal mode, they are interacting and responding to the divine presence, which impacts the divine reality.

**Richard:** Actually, we see both these aspects of God expressed in both the East and the West, so that it might be more a difference of emphasis than of outright opposition. In the Western tradition, for instance, Meister Eckhart distinguishes between God and the Godhead. The Godhead is beyond personhood, but God is the personal expression of the Godhead. In Hinduism, you have the Brahman, which is transpersonal, but also Ishvara, who is the personal expression of Brahman. The way I make sense of this is to say that our human limitations may prevent us from knowing the metaphysics of God as God is in God's self, but we can experience God in these different modes, and they are all legitimate ways of experiencing God.

There is a quote on page 301 that expresses something along these lines. God says,

> **"I manifest Myself to you in a limited way. Each particular manifestation is limited. You should never assume that this simple conversational Person is all there is to Me. I also light the stars and move the heavens, I generate matter and motion, I draw life forward toward its end, and many more things."**

So, the conversational God with whom you are talking in the book is not the whole of what God is, but God as filtered through your particular personality and understanding of things.

**Jerry:** Not remotely the whole. God gave me the title of the book *God: An Autobiography* but, because of what you are saying now, Richard, I added the subtitle, *As Told to a Philosopher*, because we do not have God on tape. We have God, as reported by me, and I am the philosopher. We have God, as Jerry Martin heard it, and it was clear from the beginning that I asked my own questions. There is no question about the Catholic Church or the Pope, for example. If I were Catholic, there certainly would have been those questions. If I had been born in India or China, I would have had quite a different range of questions. What God says is in answer to the questions I asked.

**Richard:** Would you say that what God was able to say to you was limited by the kinds of questions you asked?

**Jerry:** God could say whatever God wanted, and sometimes did. But usually God wanted to start with questions I had. I was told to ask what I most wanted to know. Had I asked different questions, I would have gotten different answers. Sometimes God says, "Bad question, ask this other thing," or just corrects the question or invalid concepts. At one point, I worried- where do you go to get new concepts? God is clearly working with my experiential and conceptual equipment. If I had different equipment, we would have a different transcript here. It might be that the transcript would be completely compatible with what God has told me, but it would look rather different. The words would be different, the topics would develop differently, and it would include a somewhat different assortment of topics. So, I take it, just from my experience—all I can do is generalize from my experience—that this is, roughly speaking, what happened to Jeremiah and, roughly speaking, what happened to Ramakrishna or the writers of the Upanishads, and Lao Tzu, and so forth. They are all receiving through their receptors and initiating their own inquiries or following their own intuitions, and this is the only way for communication with God to work, as God explains in these chapters we are now discussing.

God uses the resources of a particular culture to communicate and to actualize part of the divine reality, the divine self. So it could very well be that in the revelations to Jerry Martin, God is actualizing an aspect of the divine self not previously actualized because we are at a unique point in history that is different from past points. Human consciousness is now different, and the cultural and technological resources are different. That is all in the discussions of the nature of revelation, and they very much relate to these chapters on what God is doing with the people of India and the people of China in their diverse modes with the Confucianists, the Daoists, and so on. Factors of revelation, enlightenment, or whatever larger term you want to put on divine communications, affect all of these sacred texts and cultural traditions. These should not be thought of as limitations so much as empowerments—because of Daoist experiences and affinities, we can all learn something new.

**Richard:** This is a fascinating question—what is the nature of revelation? We touched upon some of these questions in our second dialogue.

Getting back to the relationship between Eastern and Western religions, another distinction we often find between the East and West has to do with worldly engagement. The Western religions call us to engagement in the world whereas the Eastern religions seem to emphasize detachment from worldly engagement. But these two emphases need not be seen as opposed to one another. There is an interesting quote on page 251 about connecting with the Atman that makes this clear…

**Jerry:** The Atman is the Self behind the self. The Western translation would be soul. The soul is distinct from your personality in this world. What would my soul be making of my life? The Atman is that Self behind the self. Well, then the story goes on from there.

**Richard:** Yes, and in Hinduism, the great religious project is for the person to realize oneself as the Atman, which is transcendent of individual, personal life. On page 251, you say to God,

> "Connecting with the Atman seems to take one out of oneself (a withdrawal) whereas Jesus' love brings something in: we have to flow into God and let God flow into us, East and West combined."
> And God responds "**Yes.**"

So these two movements of disengagement and engagement are not to be thought of as contrary to one another but as complementing one another. By disengaging enough to get in touch with what transcends our individual lives, we can better engage in individual life in the right way.

**Jerry:** That is right. There is that difference, hence the enormous emphasis on love, as well as obeying God in the Western traditions. The West also has an element of detachment: Let Thy will be done. Not my will, but Thy will be done. So, there is another way of actualizing some of these compatible phenomena, even though they are not just described but even experienced in almost opposite ways. God is coming into us; we are trying to step out of our lives and bodies into God.

**Richard:** Yes, both traditions have both, and it is a matter of emphasis. We may lead with our right foot or left foot, but both feet are needed to maintain balance.

Let us spend a moment talking about the way the metaphysical picture presented in the book corresponds with Eastern thought. I am thinking specifically of the discussions of reincarnation and the Atman, as well as the notion that everything and everyone is part of the divine. We associate these ideas more with Eastern thought than with Western thought.

**Jerry:** Yes. Those are explored as I deal with each of those traditions.

**Richard:** Let's see if we can sketch out how these ideas are presented in the book. There is, first of all, the Atman. It was unclear to me, in reading the book, at what point the individual Atman is created. There is discussion of the evolutionary emergence of human beings, but how the Atman emerges is never discussed.

**Jerry:** I think there is an implied answer because it is slightly different from the Hindu understanding, even though all of these discussions occur in the section on Hinduism. I did not realize that what comes through in *God: An Autobiography* is a slightly different conception of Atman. Here you have your Atman, I have mine, and each, in turn, is related to the divine reality. It is that Atman, or soul (to use that as a translation), that goes from one life to the next. In the next life, you will be quite a different person. You will have a different name, personality, and life situation, but it will be the same soul behind doing another enactment of itself. And that goes on across time and across worlds. That does not quite answer when the Atman comes about, but it suggests so very early that it could be there forever. That would be one conceptual possibility, or it could be when it becomes time to arrive, but that time is not quite the same thing as linear time. You do not even know how to talk about before and after.

**Richard:** What did you mean when you say, "when it becomes time…" Time for what?

**Jerry:** When it becomes time to enter a world. Of course, you have a soul that goes on to the next world and the world after that. I assume there must be a first world, or you would not need a soul. There is nothing for the soul to do. It is a very odd theoretical question whether the soul was already around. There is no first world in our ordinary sense because the linear time of this world is not the encompassing time or the only point of view or perspective of time. It may not make sense to make this world come into existence before or after this other world. The timelines may be internal to the worlds, not an overall linear framework in which we can place them.

**Richard:** Maybe we can express it this way: From a temporal perspective, the individual Atman, at one point, emerges from the being of God. That is its beginning, and over the course of a long career, which may proceed through multiple worlds, it progressively enters into closer and closer communion with God until it is finally reabsorbed into God. That would be the temporal point of view. But from a non-temporal point of view, the Atman is always situated in and united with God, and, beyond that, the God beyond God. So, in an ultimate sense, there is no beginning or end. That may be a way of thinking of it, although it's a bit hard to wrap your mind around.

**Jerry:** There are infinite worlds. So, how can there be an end? That ultimate level is very hard to conceptualize, and I have not felt the need to do so. I don't think the notion of being "reabsorbed into God" is found in the book, or the suggestion that the non-linear time dimension is more real or adequate than the linear. It is simply different.

**Richard:** One way the book's idea of the Atman differs from the traditional Hindu conception is that, as presented in your book, the Atman is growing. There is a process of development the Atman is undergoing.

**Jerry:** The word "learning" is used. The Atman is learning as it goes from one life to another. There is one point at which the outcome is remembered. It is a bit like the analogy of an actress who plays one part and then another part in different plays or the same part again and another play the following night. It is the same actress, and the actress remembers the various roles she has had and is probably learning to be a better actress. Now, if we also think of her more complex life, being an actress on stage takes part of her life, but she is also, let us say, a wife, a mother, a member of a church, and who knows what else? Of course, she is the one person engaged in these different roles, learning from each, growing from each, and the Atman, the soul that goes on from one life to the next, is acquiring these aspects, experiences, or traits. It is not clear what that residue is, other than that it is called learning, which certainly includes memory and residues of attitude or character.

**Richard:** The goal is not to break the chain of reincarnation. You are not striving to get to a point where you do not continue reincarnating. This, again, differs from the classical view we get in Eastern religion, where you are trying to escape the cycle of birth and death.

**Jerry:** Right. In the Hindu view, you are trapped on the wheel of karma. So, you have to go through it and do it over and over and over. It is dreadful. So they want liberation from the wheel of karma. None of that is in *God: An Autobiography*. There are multiple worlds, and each is deeply meaningful; each is a life that adds to the whole totality of worlds. You are doing your part in cooperation with the divine to actualize all of these many, many possibilities. Karma is mentioned, but not carefully defined. Occasionally, it is used in a key way, as if your karma seems to have something to do with your task from one life to the next. It is not to pay your penalties. It is not because you were a bad person before that, now, you will suffer or have to work it off. It is not that. Nevertheless, the phrase is used: you need to balance your life. That might mean, like a musician, you have done this kind of music, but you need to balance that out. You have rhythm down, but you need to get subtle notes in, too. So you need to balance things from one life to the next. Any life is going to be one-sided. So, there is always something left out that another life has a chance to balance.

**Richard:** On page 229, God says,

> "The key to karma is dharma. Dharma is your duty in your situation."

Can you expand on that?

**Jerry:** That is right. It is very unlike classical Hinduism, where Dharma is your social role, which is the theological foundation of the caste system. Most Hindus I know reject the caste system as a social rigidification of a valid insight. Your karma in this life, something like your task in this life is to pay attention to your Dharma by looking at your situation and figuring out what it behooves you to do in light of your being a child with these parents, being a neighbor of these neighbors, and being in this kind of political community, having these talents and not having these other talents, or having these challenges. I saw somebody on television who had a terrible temper and was led to violence. He found that working out in the gym helped. So he was working on noting his situation and the Dharma that follows. Who knows? Body chemistry can lead to losing a temper, so he now knows how to cope with that.

**Richard:** On page 311, you ask the God beyond God whether the divine self has a 'karma.' God responds,

> **"Yes, My karma, if we call it that, has to do with unfurling world after world, God after God, and tracing their steps, following their progress, sharing their burdens and hopes and sufferings."**

You then ask why it is important for you to know this, and the God beyond God says,

> **"Because this is the ultimate story, the ultimate meaning of it all. . . It is in the nature of reality that the world, the totality of worlds plus Me, is here for a purpose. There is a goal. . . The goal is completeness, connectedness, to create the many and to pull them back into the one."**

This seems to be the big, overall, picture. Out of the Atman of God arises an almost unimaginable diversity of distinct things, which then have to be brought into harmony with one another, a harmony that can itself take an infinite variety of forms. And we are all participants in this project.

**Jerry:** I gather the drawing into one is not like Plotinus, where you have to draw everything back into a single, simple unity, but like what you just said, Richard, as harmony. It is as though you have got a bunch of people showing up with musical instruments, and now you have to make music that actually fits rather than just being a cacophony. An awful lot of life in the world is a cacophony. It is a great bunch of people stridently doing different things, at odds with one another, and contending in everything from opinions to actions to institutions and lifestyles. The goal is to have them somehow in harmony with one another. When they are in harmony with one another, the diversity becomes very rich, very fulfilled, and the totality is very rich and fulfilled. In the totality and the unity of the simple one, there is not a whole lot of actualization of value. But in these multiple worlds, with rich diversity and all these different souls enacting lives, to the extent one can bring them into some kind of harmony, one is getting somewhere that matters.

One of the passages in this section compares it to a kind of music group. I am not enough of a musician to do this myself, but I have seen where they come together, each bringing their own instruments, and I thought it was quite a phenomenon. One starts a tune or something, and the others kind of play on it. Sometimes taking turns with regard to who is doing the lead and developing the music around them. Sometimes it is a jazz version, but I have heard other versions that are not. These various instruments start coming together rather spontaneously, though, often, the people know each other. But they start creating—creating because they are not enacting a score or doing something that has already been created. They are creating new music in harmony with one another, knowing how to play off one another. That is a talent- if only we can learn in life how to successfully play off one another.

**Richard:** This discussion of harmony leads us to the treatment of Chinese religion in the book. The book points out that the idea of harmony is at the core of Chinese religion. We see it in Daoism.

The yin and the yang must be brought into harmony. We see a similar pursuit of harmony in Confucianism, where the focus is on harmony in human relations.

**Jerry:** That would be a lot like the Karma is Dharma line in which Confucius emphasizes one's social roles, the seven sacred relationships. If you enact those properly, then you have social harmony.

**Richard:** As Confucius sees it, the social role is not simply the role assigned to you by society, but the role you must play in order for relationships to achieve their good. The question then becomes: What kind of person does one have to be to achieve harmonious relations? How must one be constituted *inwardly*?

And this, perhaps, leads us back to Hinduism. On page 199, God says,

> "**The people of India received more truly and clearly than anyone that the way to reach Me is through the inside, that I am the Ur-consciousness of each individual's consciousness.**"

**Jerry:** Yes. God says, here, that it is a revolutionary discovery not just in human development but in God's development as well. We must remember that with each of these, God is discovering something about the divine self as people react differently. Through the Chinese, God discovered Godself as cosmic harmony, as a kind of divine hum to the universe. Here, God is discovering the divine self as connected in this extremely intimate way, that almost amounts to pure identity, to the individual's most intimate aspect. God's most intimate aspect and the individual's most intimate aspect interact so closely that it is almost, according to *God: An Autobiography*, mistaken for an identity. It is not quite an identity, but it is this extremely close affinity.

**Richard:** We have spoken a lot about the need for balance. It is almost as if the focus on one's inner identity with God in the Eastern religions balances out the vision of God as a transcendent lawgiver in the Western religions. If we think of these two as balancing each other out rather than opposing each other, we get the idea that it is through experiencing God in an inward way that we are better able to live in accordance with the imperatives—or 'laws'—of God in an outward way.

This gets expressed on page 202, where God talks about the importance of 'detachment.' God says,

> **"What detachment does is to put you on My side of the great lines (the great divide). There is a physical reality and you can identify with that, and there is a divine reality and you can identify with that—if you detach from things first. You cannot do your full work in conjunction with me without detachment."**

**Jerry:** Good point. Yes. It is emphasized in the Bhagavad Gita.

**Richard:** As Hinduism presents it, a central problem of human life is that people become attached to finite things, which leads to greed, discord, violence, etc. It also leads to a radical insecurity, because to try to secure yourself through what is itself insecure is like clinging to a sinking boat to keep yourself from drowning.

**Jerry:** That is the Buddhist insight. What you just said could be stated as the essence of Buddhism, that we cling to things that are themselves insubstantial.

**Richard:** So, to live healthily we must overcome our attachment to fleeting things and come to recognize our embeddedness in the divine. This is one of the great insights of the Eastern religions. But we can now couple this with the message of Western religion: the purpose of detachment is not to become disengaged from the world. Its purpose is to allow us to live more fully and healthily within it.

**Jerry:** Yes, that is exactly right, Richard. Detachment allows us to engage in the world for divine purposes rather than acting out of our own ego, greed, and lust. These very words about detachment are said in the famous text of the Bhagavad Gita in the context of convincing Arjuna to fight in the battle.

**Richard:** Yes, this is Arjuna's dharma; he must fulfill his dharma.

**Jerry:** Yes, exactly. When you fight, whether you will win or not is not in your hands. While trying to win, it is not as though you want to appropriate the victory as a kind of possession at the end. That is not the goal. It is to do your duty and be in partnership with the divine represented here by Krishna.

**Richard:** The reason to fight is to achieve the good; it is not for self-aggrandizement. The fight is for a better, more ideal, more harmonious world. This is why the Bhagavad Gita became such a favorite text of Gandhi. He strongly believed that spiritual awareness must express itself through engagement with the world, to make the world a better place.

In this context, we see some criticism in the book of Shankara's Advaita Vedanta, which looks upon the finite world as illusory. On page 211, God says,

> **"Shankara was a great man and understood in great depth what he understood, but what he understood was extremely one-sided."**

**Jerry:** Yes. He veered off too far toward what in the West we would call a monistic idealism, too far in the direction of the world not being real. The God of *God: An Autobiography* constantly corrects that idea about the world in various contexts. The world is not an illusion. It is quite real. There are real consequences to engaging in the world. There is not a divine play going on for idle amusement. The world is quite real. Suffering is real. Victory and loss are real. The Nazis killing people is real, and our defeating the Nazis is real.

Shankara understood, very deeply, the one truth you were articulating from the book, Richard, the deep way in which the self and the divine are intimately related. Our task is to honor that relationship and to live out that relationship, and not to be pulled away. The world is real, but it also offers all these temptations, snares, and delusions. So the fundamental truth that Shankara understood is that, no, in terms of life priorities, grabbing onto things around you is not, "real." It is a very low priority or anti-priority because it gets in the way of what you should be doing. It gets in the way of doing your duty in the world, your proper Dharma.

**Richard:** A basic theme running through the book is that the world is real. The concreteness, the granularity of reality, is not something we should try to escape. It is where the action is, where the rubber meets the road. Even the God beyond God is not adequate, but only becomes adequate through the creation of the finite world, where we are called to fulfill our Dharma and fight the good fight.

We have not talked a lot about Buddhism. I was surprised by what seemed to me a slightly dismissive attitude toward Buddhism in the book.

**Jerry:** God says it was not a major revelation. The Buddha was a remarkable individual, and he had a wonderful message in terms of compassion, especially in that concept of the bodhisattva, where even the most actualized persons, who is ready to do what Buddha thinks the aim of life should be, which is to move off into Nirvana, sacrifice themselves to stay in the world until every other single person achieves Nirvana. Well, that is a wonderful image and lesson, but God completely rejects the Buddhist version of the way in which the world is not real, "not real" is probably an overstatement, as it is for the Hindus, also. The whole chain of causation that the Buddha speaks of is Buddha's effort to solve the problem of suffering. Suffering is caused by attachment to things. Things are themselves, he decides, ephemeral. They are not self-sustaining, and as soon as you see they are ephemeral, you will not suffer anymore. Well, God does not think they are ephemeral. Buddha has no sense of the gritty nature of reality, of this as being the arena in which everything counts. There is actual work to do in this world, not just to escape it, to rise above it, or to see it in a different way as radically less real and unsustaining. That does not understand the nature of the world and of our role in the world which is, I take it, the problem here.

**Richard:** Although the Mahayana strain of Buddhism, which emphasizes the role of the bodhisattva in going out into the world to relieve suffering, does seem to bring us back to engagement with the world. I know many people who find great spiritual profundity in Buddhism. They don't see it as promoting disengagement but as helping us get in touch with what the Mahayana tradition calls our 'Buddha nature'—that in us that transcends attachments—so that we can live in the world in a peaceful and harmonious way.

**Jerry:** Here, as in the other religions, I did not pray about later developments. I prayed about the early text, the things closest to the revelation, in this case, the Pali canon. This is the Buddha's foundational, revelatory, or enlightenment text. There are then all these developments, which I did not go into. I became aware of the bodhisattvas, but I take it, Richard, that everything you said is one part of Buddhism that God endorsed. God rejects the metaphysics. God thinks the lesson of compassion is powerful, and that Buddha had such a fine sensibility that he virtually felt everybody else's suffering. We *talk* about feeling your pain. He really *did* feel people's pain—and looked to do something about it.

**Richard:** Both Buddha and Jesus are deeply connected to the suffering of humanity and both try to find ways to heal it. Perhaps next time we'll talk more fully about the way the Eastern and Western religions may be seen as balancing each other out. The book suggests that we need this balance in order for religion to be healthy. Where this balance is missing, we get a perversion of religion, a distortion with pernicious consequences.

**Jerry:** Yes, because each one, in a sense, grabs on to one big truth, one fundamental truth, and develops that to the nth degree.

**Richard:** This reminds me of the preface to Sherwood Anderson's *Winesburg, Ohio*. He writes of sitting in bed and seeing a great swarm of grotesque faces pass before his mind's eye. He asks himself the reason for their grotesqueness. He finally realizes that it is due to their having seized hold of one truth to the exclusion of all others. Maybe the historical religions have had something of this grotesqueness about them as well.

**Jerry:** Yes. Well, it is a natural human tendency. Thank you, Richard. Fascinating discussion.

# 10. The Essential Project of the Divine

**Dr. Richard Oxenberg** In our last couple of sessions we've looked at the Western and Eastern religions and examined some of their differences. Of course, one of the basic themes of the book is that all the religions are expressions of one divine project and should ultimately be seen as complementary. I thought that today we would try to identify that project and discuss how the different religions might be seen as varying expressions of it.

**Dr. Jerry L. Martin** Yes. What puzzled me at the beginning when I was told to read these foundational scriptures of different traditions was, why? What are we doing here? What will we learn? It becomes much clearer as the story unfolds how the divine manifests Godself in these multiple ways.

**Richard:** We've spoken a lot about harmony. A major theme of the book is that there can be a harmony between the different religions. We should see them, not as rivals and competitors, but as harmonious and complementary. They are different pieces of a greater puzzle.

**Jerry:** Yes, and it is different from some other similarly nice understandings because it does not require that they all say the same thing, and it explains why it is important and valuable that they do not all say the same thing. Most people try to echo each other with this intuitive sense that you have when you do a serious study of the religions that they all contain divinely inspired insights. Yet, you look up close, and each one has its own quite different vocabulary, rituals, and theologies.

**Richard:** And different emphases. Almost everything can be found in each one of them if you look hard enough but emphasized differently.

**Jerry:** Different emphases. Yes, that is right. Very much emphasized differently.

**Richard:** I thought we might begin today by looking again at a quote we've discussed before. As I've said, I tend to see this quote as at the very center of the book. You are speaking to what the book calls the 'Atman of God,' which the book also calls 'the God beyond God'…

**Jerry:** As you pointed out, at the beginning of the book and the beginning of the story of God with creation, it is the God before the world is created, when there is not much description to God. You nicely picked up on this question- what is going on with that, and why is the God beyond God creating and thereby entering our world, and as it turns out, other worlds as well?

**Richard:** On page 31, The Atman of God says,

> **"This is the ultimate story, the ultimate meaning of it all. I have a project to complete… It is in the nature of reality that the world, the totality of worlds plus Me, is here for a purpose. There is a goal."**
>
> And you ask, "What is the goal?" A pertinent question!

## THE ESSENTIAL PROJECT OF THE DIVINE

**Jerry:** Yes. That is very pertinent, what is the big story? I kept wanting to know what the purpose of all this was.

**Richard:** The God beyond God says,

> **"The goal is completeness, connectedness, to create the many and to pull them back into the one."** This is the big, grand project.

**Jerry:** It is the purpose of it all.

**Richard:** It is rooted in a basic metaphysical vision: There is an original Oneness that expresses itself in a vast multiplicity of more limited forms. This results in the Many emerging out of the One, which we may think of as 'the creation.' But this very process of creation presents a problem and a challenge, a goal that needs to be pursued—of bringing this great multiplicity into harmony with itself, a harmony that is possible precisely because the multiplicity is an expression of an underlying Oneness.

**Jerry:** I want to add here that the motive for God's expressing the divine self is to be real. It is not just God wishing for an audience like an unemployed actor. It is to be real because that primal state of the divine is sometimes described as a Nothingness. It is a Nothingness full of potentiality, but there is not much going on there. It seems placid, quiet, and not quite real. You are right; the worlds are created, and multiplicity is created for the God beyond God to become real. The only way to become real is to become particular in a world. You are going on, Richard, in a way that seems quite right. There is an actualization of the divine, but there are now challenges and problems.

**Richard:** What we learn throughout the book is that what is meant by "pulling them back into the one" is not the collapsing of the multiplicity into the same oneness that gave birth to it. Rather, the particulars are to become aware of themselves as united with the One while retaining their particularity. It is this that allows the particulars, while remaining particulars, to harmonize with one another.

**Jerry:** Yes, exactly. I often picture when we look at those kinds of passages as if everybody brings their own instruments to some local town event, maybe the annual town fair or something like that. Some of the instruments are not really what we think of as instruments at all. Somebody is playing a saw or tapping on bottles of water and slapping their knees. One has to have everybody bring their "instruments" together. You have the diversity- everybody has their own interesting equipment. Now, how do you make music out of it? How do you put it together into something that actually is harmonious and that makes sense? That is the challenge of a world because the world has that kind of diversity and even more. I imagine townspeople who are mainly well-intentioned, but of course, some of the people who are showing up are not well-intentioned. Their goal is to frustrate. So the challenge of a world is to make some harmony out of all that extreme diversity and multiplicity of motives.

**Richard:** You have to maintain two 'awarenesses' at the same time. You have to be aware of your own particularity. If you are playing the saw, you have to know how to play the saw. You also have to be aware of the overarching context in which you are expressing that particularity so that it can blend in with all the other particularities. That becomes the great challenge, and of course, that is where we run into problems, where various particulars do not blend in, and now we have issues.

Applying this to religion, we might say that the world's various religions emerge with a central goal of bringing the particulars—particular human beings—into awareness of, and harmony with, the whole. That is what each religion, in its own way, is about. They each provide a vision of the whole, but they each remain particular, and their vision of the whole is limited by their particularity, a limitation they often fail to realize.

**Jerry:** When that happens, they mistake themselves for the whole. They think they have all the truth, that they are the whole story of the divine. Then you have this conflict of dogmatisms, each one claiming to be the only truth. Other beliefs are denounced as falsehood, heresy, or the enemy. Part of what *God: An Autobiography* does is explain that each truth has picked up on one aspect of the divine and is bringing it to actualization as one particular expression of the divine. Now, at our point in time, in light of *God: An Autobiography*, we have the challenge of what to make of the many ways of being—of cultures, of individuals, and of religions. As you said at the beginning, Richard, now we have a problem. We have a diversity of people, cultures, and religions, but now we have the problem that they are often in conflict, and often it is not even well-intentioned conflict.

**Richard:** And part of the problem pertains to the limitations of revelation itself. God is limited in the divine capacity to reveal Godself by the limitations of those *to whom* God is revealing the divine self—just as the electromagnetic spectrum can only reveal itself to our senses in accordance with what our particular senses can pick up. There is a big spectrum beyond what our senses can register.

**Jerry:** Yes. Some other creatures, like bats or dogs with their acute hearing, can register things that we do not register. We can say something similar about revelation. Each different culture, each different epoch, can pick up different things about the divine which accounts for the great diversity of religion. Now we can see that.

One tends to talk in terms of limitations, and God certainly does talk in those terms, but it is also something like empowerments. Any one mode of music is limited to that mode of music. A string quartet can only do what string quartets do. That is how to empower that kind of music. Things can only become actual through these particular mediums. What God says about cultures is that each culture has certain talents, concepts, and affinities that evoke an aspect of God. I am not using language from the book exactly, but the culture evokes an aspect of the divine.

**Richard:** An interesting twist in the book, which goes hand in hand with what we've been saying about revelation, is that God becomes aware of God only as the human being becomes aware of God.

**Jerry:** Human beings evoke that aspect of the divine, which only at that moment becomes actualized and, being actualized, comes to God's attention.

**Richard:** So what we're calling revelation is not quite as simple as one person giving information to another. It is a process of discovery. The human being discovers God, and the divine discovers Godself through that discovery.

A quote on page 301 speaks of the limitations of revelation. God says,

> "I manifest Myself to you in a limited way. Each particular manifestation is limited. You should never assume that this simple conversational Person is all there is to Me. I also light the stars and move the heavens, I generate matter and motion, I draw life forward toward its end, and many more things."

In effect, in the book we are getting a narrow band of the spectrum of what God is in God's totality. We should not take this as a definitive view of God, but as one window into what God is.

## THE ESSENTIAL PROJECT OF THE DIVINE

**Jerry:** It may be definitive in the sense of entirely truthful without it being the only truth about God. We can speak of limitations, but not in a way that casts doubt on this report of aspects of the divine reality. However, there are other ways of telling God's story that God did not share with me that have equal validity.

**Richard:** It is one window. It's as if there are many different windows through which we can look to see different aspects of the divine. They are all valid in themselves, but they are all limited, and we need to be aware of both these things.

Once again, the quote from page 90 expresses this,

> "I came to all peoples, but arrived in different guises. I came to the American Indians as the Great Spirit, to the Moslems as Allah, and so on. I came to the Hindus in many forms, and hence their many stories."

So, as you've been saying, it's not that each of the religions is the same. The Great Spirit is not Brahman, and Brahman is not Allah. But they are each a window into a divine truth that both includes and transcends all of them.

**Jerry:** That aspect of the divine becomes real or actualized at the time of the revelation or through the revelation.

**Richard:** That is also an important point. It's not simply that the different religions are limited windows into a greater whole, such that, if we could only come to know that greater whole we could do away with the many windows. Rather, each window has its own value, its own way in which the divine-human relation is actualized. The different religions are, so to speak, different dances that humans can do with the divine, and each dance has its own beauty, its own grace, and its own validity.

**Jerry:** That is one metaphor. Each dance would express one aspect of the divine, and there will be new dances that express new emerging aspects of the divine. This is not a static picture at all. So it is hard to know what metaphor to use. It is better to think of a dynamic metaphor than a static one. In a static image, we are looking through a window as if were we to stick our heads out far enough, we could see all 360 degrees. No, it is not like that. The reality of God is emerging through these interactions, through these reactions of cultures, so God is expressing and actualizing God's self. The cultures are receptive to parts and are reacting to aspects of God's self that God had not realized. God started giving laws to the ancient people of Israel and became a lawgiver. That was a new thing. God sets norms in every culture, but not necessarily as Ten Commandments. God discovered that aspect of God's reality.

**Richard:** Yes, and, as we noted earlier, God says to you on page 243,

> **"You relate to me personally, and see other revelations as glosses on that experience. But they could just as well see your relation to a personal God as a gloss on Brahman or Buddha or the Tao."**

In other words, it is not that one is more valid than the other; each of them is valid.

**Jerry:** Completely valid, presumably, or valid enough as genuine expressions of the divine. The book is a dialogue between God and me. I pray about a sacred text, and then I ask God, what does this mean? What were You doing then? I do not do anything Daoist myself other than read the text and pray, asking: What does this mean? What was going on, and what was God doing vis-a-vis the Daoist or the Buddhist? It is difficult because of the limitations of empathy. How much empathy would it take for one person to think that this personal God, as experienced by Jerry and many other people, and central to certain major religions, is not at all the only aspect of the divine? It may not be the most important aspect of the divine, but there is an equally valid tradition saying other important things and we would be off track if we overdid the personal side. Nevertheless, at some point in the development of most religions, whatever their emphasis, they allow some stream of thinking about a personal dimension to the divine.

**Richard:** God is both personal and transpersonal. It's not a matter of either/or but both/and.

**Jerry:** Both/and—exactly!

**Richard:** And as we said earlier, what seem at first to be major differences often turn out to be differences in emphasis. You can find mystical union in Western religion, but that is not what is emphasized. What is emphasized is the person-to-person relationship. And you can find a person-to-person approach in the East, but that is not what is emphasized. Eastern religion emphasizes transpersonal union. What it seems we have to say is that the actual reality of the divine is beyond both these ways of experiencing God. God is capable of manifesting the divine self in both ways but is not fully expressed in either of them.

**Jerry:** Yes. I tend not to talk that way, but it is for philosophical reasons. Some philosophers like to postulate that, behind phenomena, there is some other reality that transcends or is otherwise quite different from its phenomenal manifestations. And, in this way of thinking, this more fundamental reality either does not actually have the qualities manifested or it has them fully actual prior to their manifestation. You and I have already discussed the understanding that they were not already there. The divine has all these potentials, but we see it from the side where the "potentials" appear to people. These *are* the actualization of the divine. The religions are apprehending them and what is apprehended *is* the divine. The divine actually *has* these multiple aspects. It is not that they are hints or partial clues about something else. What would that other thing be? That is a quandary prominent from the ancient skeptical debates and the way some modern philosophers talk. Similarly, people can emphasize either the validity and actualization of the revelations or their limitations and culture-boundedness. Both are true, of course, but I find the first emphasis more theologically revealing.

**Richard:** I'm trying to get a sense for how it all fits together. Looking at the big picture, we first have what the book calls 'the Atman of God,' which the book tells us is at least somewhat similar to what Hinduism calls 'Brahman.' On page 296, for instance, you write,

> "I was thinking the God beyond God might be like an impersonal Brahman."
> And God responds, **"Yes, it is complex, but it is connected."**

It occurs to me that this is important from a spiritual point of view. The God of this world is limited in a number of ways. God is subject to suffering, subject to ignorance, and we're even told that there are some aspects of God that might even be seen as evil, or as having the potential for evil. But this is not true of the God beyond God.

**Jerry:** Yes, although we have to remind ourselves that the God in this world is identical to the God beyond God. It is the God beyond God actualized, and hence made fully real, in a world.

**Richard:** It is a manifestation of the God beyond God.

**Jerry:** It is an *actualization* of the God beyond God. Just as the God beyond God, it is not yet actualized. It is sort of nothing, though not an empty nothing. It is important to remember that the God we are relating to in this world is not a second being. We are relating to the God beyond God as It enters this world.

**Richard:** Yes, but there is a nuance here that I think we need to attend to. There is a difference between the God of this world and the God beyond God, even though the former is, so to speak, ontologically embedded in the latter. The God of this world is temporal and developing whereas the God beyond God is eternal. For instance, on page 73 we read of the God beyond God:

> "**There was a Self, timeless, without reflection, still and at peace, like calm waters, lucid, not nothing, but not something either.**" Then on 311, we have the God beyond God described as, "**calm, dispassionate, quiet, tranquil, serene, blissful.**"

And, though the emergent God, the God of this world, may be thought of as an actualization of the God beyond God, it is not as if the latter simply transforms into the former. The "calm, dispassionate, quiet, tranquil, serene, blissful" God beyond God is still present; in fact you speak to it in the book. We can get in touch with it. We think of the emergence of this world in temporal terms, but the book makes clear that, in an ultimate sense, everything is happening simultaneously. So the God beyond God is still here, now, as the eternal reality underlying temporal reality.

**Jerry:** There is still linear time. Linear time—time in the sense of before-and-after—is perfectly real. As we live our lives and God develops, that is all perfectly real. On the other hand, there is another dimension and way of looking at it where the times are all simultaneous, and that perspective is, well, I started to say more real, but that is not right. They are each real in their own different ways. You just need to understand which time sense you are talking about. It is really true that Caesar crossed the Rubicon before he was assassinated, even though, in a history book, we can read about both events on the same page.

**Richard:** Yes, and spiritually, we need both these points of view, the eternal and the temporal. The eternal adds something to the temporal. For instance, on 184, speaking of the God beyond God, we read:

> "It is true that, in that mode or dimension, evil cannot strike. There is no evil in the 'world' of the God beyond God."

This implies that what we take to be evil is not ontologically fundamental. It is a product of the manifestation, or the creation, of the many out of the One, but it is not a feature of the One itself.

**Jerry:** However, when you say it that way, "ontologically," it seems you are reversing something I keep emphasizing: the God beyond God is not quite real in that mode. Of course, there is no evil there. It is placid. Nothing is going on there. There is no good either. There is no beauty. To actualize, which would suggest becoming *more* real, God must enter a world. The God in the world is, therefore, more real than the God sitting back, vaguely aware of the possibility of becoming real. It is blissful, it is perfect only because nothing is happening.

**Richard:** But I'm not sure that to say it is beyond evil implies that it is also beyond good. I think back to the quote on page 312 that says that the aim of creation is to create the many and bring them back into the one. If it were not for the fact that the original One is at peace, calm, and beyond evil, it would not resolve anything to bring the creation back into the One. In other words, there is something about bringing it all back into oneness that resolves the problems caused by the creation of the many. There is a quality of peace, even bliss, to the One that lends itself to the many when the many get in touch with it.

**Jerry:** The quality that is so wonderful in the resolution is harmony. There is no harmony back in the God beyond God because there is no multiplicity. You have to have all those instruments come to the town meeting and have those problems before you can have the solution.

**Richard:** But you also cannot have harmony unless there is unity. All the parts must be able to fit together. One can imagine irresolvable chaos emerging out of some primordial 'Big Bang'—jagged pieces that can't fit together harmoniously. Then there would only be, to use Hobbes' saying, "a war of all against all," a churning chaos, discordant with itself.

There must be an ontological potential for harmony. It's true that harmony requires that there be multiplicity, but it also requires that the multiplicity be such that the multiplicitous pieces can come together into a greater and more harmonious whole. And this potential for harmony—at least as I've come to think of it—has its basis in the unity of the God beyond God.

**Jerry:** I think of this a little more dialectically, that we go from an extremely undeveloped God beyond God to God's actualizing God's self in multiple worlds and then having the problems you rightly describe. Because a world has limitations and elements of decline built right into it—of incompleteness, conflict, and of course also the elephant you emphasize, Richard, a constant factor that the divine is in this world, and its multiple aspects are in this world, moving it toward harmony. The most real state would not be the primal state where we started; it would be the final state with the full actualization of harmony.

**Richard:** Yes, and I think the word 'dialectic' here is a good one. The way I would put it is that the potential for harmony is a function of a dialectic between the multiplicity of the creation and the unity of the God beyond God. Harmony requires both.

And this may be a way of understanding the complementarity of Eastern and Western religion as well. In many ways, the East emphasizes unity and the West emphasizes multiplicity. The East emphasizes the One and the West emphasizes the Many. But we need both for a complete picture.

**Jerry:** Yes. Fair enough.

**Richard:** We can pursue this further by looking at a quote from page 184. God says,

> **"Reality wants to be embodied. In this respect, philosophical traditions that derive from Plato, Aristotle, Plotinus get it wrong. The material object does not 'fall beneath' the perfect 'form;' it actualizes it."**

This is very much what you've been saying. But God continues,

> **"That (material existence) does subject it to limitations—hence the sense of a 'fall from grace'—which subjects it to erosion, destruction, and in more complex forms, disease, dysfunction, and in human beings, death suffering and evil."**

It is just this 'fall from grace'—our subjection to erosion, destruction, disease, dysfunction, death, suffering, and evil—that needs to be resolved. I would suggest that, at a spiritual level, we resolve it through getting in touch with that within us that is not subject to erosion, destruction, dysfunction, death, suffering, and evil—which in your book is called the God beyond God. The aim is not to lose ourselves in the eternity of the God beyond God, but to ground ourselves in it. It is just such grounding that allows us to live out our particularity in peace and grace. I think the God beyond God corresponds, in many ways, to what in Buddhism is called 'emptiness,' *sunyata*.

It's interesting to speculate why the creation of the many should result in such negativity. As I've come to understand it, it's because the particular is not self-sustaining; it requires connection with the whole in order to be sustained. So, its very particularity, which distinguishes it from the whole that sustains it, is also something of a threat to it. It is in danger, or can feel itself to be in danger, of being severed from the whole that sustains it.

**Jerry:** I do not think that vocabulary came into the dialogues with God. What did come in was the nature of material reality. To be actualized is to be material. It is not as if God could have come into a perfect spiritual world. We would have had the problem that God starts out not being actualized. To be actualized is to go into a particular world. God does not make up the laws of nature. Entropy is built into what it is to be a material world, and entropy includes all these organic problems of aging. It is a world that has to be real and have these problems. What you are talking about in terms of the particularity, that incompleteness, does seem to be in the book. We are looking for a connection between the divine and our particularity. While the real world actualizes us, it presents us with the problem of connectedness. What is our relation to the whole? What is our relation to one another? That is a key element here.

**Richard:** A question I have asked myself, apart from reading your book, is about something we often take for granted: Why do we *care* that we die? Why should there be any distress over death? What does it say about the nature of the life urge within us that we do not want to die? Where does it come from—this urgent desire not to die?

We want to be eternal and whole but, at the same time—as you keep pointing out—we need to be embodied and limited in order to be fully actual. And so there is a paradox or ambiguity inherent to our very being, inherent, perhaps, to being itself. On the one hand, we need our particularity in order to be fully actual; on the other hand, our particularization limits us in a way that our life urge struggles against. Perhaps this is why religion is necessary. It opens us to communion with the whole that we have been severed from in our particularization.

**Jerry:** There is more to reality than this finite temporal horizon that demarcates our birth and death. That is not the total picture. There is more happening right here and now than that sense of it as short and fleeting. One can get that other perspective. I do not think the word "eternal" is used here, but it is often used in these kinds of discussions. You might say that our own soul's destiny has this other perspective where the key thing is not the day we are born or the day we die; it is each and every moment that has its own deep, deep, deep importance in relation to the divine.

**Richard:** Yes, and it takes some doing for us to become aware of that other perspective.

**Jerry:** As you point out, we are thrown into this world with our limitations. I was given a vision early of the life force rising up through all of nature and the tiers of nature. The most fundamental biological urges are always present, even as we move up through tiers looking for love, beauty, and wisdom. Even as we move up, the life force expresses itself in a kind of teleological way. It is moving up towards these higher values, but it is always rooted in nature all the way down to basic biological urges. It is the life force expressing itself. That is how we are in this world. So, at the end of those life forces, it is as if everything collapses like a house of cards. The noble collapses along with the basic biological. Except, there is another, larger perspective that is hard for us to tap into, but it is possible to do so.

**Richard:** It is hard to tap into, as you point out, because we also want and need to maintain our particularity. There is a quote on page 53 that pertains to this, about the ego. It is the ego that particularizes us. Ego is the Latin for "I." So, my ego is my I, and your ego is your I, and we could not be different particularities, different particular people, unless we had different egos, different I's. But the ego can become wrapped up in itself and closed off from the rest of reality, perhaps it even has a tendency to do so. As we read on page 53, God says,

> **"Ego is destructive, separatist, defiant of My will, self-satisfied and self-lustful."**

So, the ego's particularization can lead to it becoming 'separatist,' and this becomes a problem.

**Jerry:** We could not survive well if we did not have some ego strength. However, it can become perverse and defiant—rather than just paying attention to one's own business, which would be the proper purview of the I or the ego, it becomes defiant and wants to break norms and do the wrong thing. That is also part of this ego's assertiveness. It is not just self-interest that can lead one to predation of one's neighbors. It is more perverse than that. It is the ego's dramatic, willful self-assertion.

**Richard:** Yes, it is almost as if the ego—or perhaps we should say the 'separatist' ego—wants to make itself God. It wants to be God in its own 'ego-ness,' its own particularity. It does not want to submit to anything beyond itself. The book speaks of the importance of surrender and sacrifice in order to come into touch with the divine. But the separatist ego is defiant of this. It does not want to submit; it wants to be in charge.

**Jerry:** It would rather boss other people around and have them submit to the person's ego.

**Richard:** And yet the separatist ego's notion that it might be capable of existing on its own, that it might be able to make itself the basis of its own existence, is really an illusion. It is a metaphysical, ontological illusion because the ego is constantly being sustained by the greater life force that it rests in, that is the basis of its own being.

**Jerry:** Indeed, everything down to one's friends, neighbors, the people you buy your groceries from, and the ecosystem, the global economy, and the social system, all the way up to the divine, energizes the whole. All of these are the forces behind one's own existence.

**Richard:** And it is this problem that all the religions, in their various ways, seem to be trying to address. They create systems, rituals, practices, doctrines designed to help the ego get beyond its sense of ontological isolation, which gives rise to its separatist project, its endeavor to make itself self-sufficient and self-contained. In some sense, all the religions are various ways of dealing with this perverse condition that the ego, in its particularization, is almost naturally inclined to fall into.

**Jerry:** That is right. None of the religions celebrates the aggressive self appropriating ego. They all look to rise above that because they all think that ultimately there is something more fundamental in reality than your ego and mind.

## THE ESSENTIAL PROJECT OF THE DIVINE

**Richard:** This comes to be the real meaning of sacrifice, as the book presents it. Interestingly, even the God beyond God is engaged in sacrifice. On page 305, you say,

> "Lord, is entering the world a sacrifice for You?"
> The God beyond God responds, "**Yes, I am in eternal peace. Then I erupt into the world.**"

As we know from reading the creation passages, this eruption is not entirely peaceful. At first, it is lonely and disruptive.

**Jerry:** And God does not know what to do. God is just trying to figure out God's role and how to do it. It is chaos all around God at that stage.

**Richard:** Then you say, "Lord isn't the core meaning of sacrifice its etymological meaning, to make sacred, make holy, mark off for God, surrender to God?"

> God responds, "**Yes, this last is it.**"
> Then you say, "How does entering the world involve surrendering to God? I don't know if this is You or me talking, Lord, but what I get is this: Entering the world is to begin to desire, and desire is essentially a craving for possession, or for acquiring experience for the self. It is inherently selfish in this sense. One enters the world of desire and yet must renounce it and give it up to God at the same time."
> And God responds, "**That is correct.**"

So, there is a dialectic that must go on between desire and sacrifice. On the one hand, we need to enter the world of desire, which is the world of the ego. Otherwise, we remain in the amorphous soup of pure potentiality. On the other hand, while we are living in this world of desire, we have to sacrifice. We have to be willing to sacrifice in order to connect with that which is beyond the ego.

**Jerry:** Yes and of course, part of that problematic of desire is that love is an aspect of desire or a type of desire. Love is also, in some sense, the essential positive force in the universe. Without desire, no love. Some desires can be a problem, of course, in human love relationships. You may love a beautiful woman, and then you want to dominate her, and maybe even crush her spirit to put her in your back pocket. You see dramas of this sort all the time, of that lustful love. I am not using lustful just in the sexual sense, but what you read from God a moment ago, God is also subject to desire, the desire to appropriate experiences for oneself and to own the one loved.

That is a sacrifice for God as well because, in this world, we have that God of desire. Not much is going on at the level of the God beyond God, but it is peaceful and fine. There is nothing wrong there, and no problems other than not quite being real. Then the divine goes into a world, and God too is now part of all this trouble, including decline, entropy, the laws of nature, and the life of desire. God too, can get frustrated. For example, when people disobey. God loves and loves in a very active way. When people have bad things happen to them, God suffers right along with them. Also, when they turn bad, like a parent seeing their child become a drug dealer, it is a heartbreaking experience. God's heart breaks, too. It is a very dramatic sacrifice for God to come into the world because that is the only way to have that process work and come out with that harmony we are talking about. God must enter and relate to the cultures and then deal with their clashes. This is the task God takes on.

**Richard:** So, we might say that the ultimate spiritual aim is to learn to desire, and love, properly.

**Jerry:** Yes, that is a good way to put it.

## THE ESSENTIAL PROJECT OF THE DIVINE

**Richard:** This reminds me of the Second Noble Truth of Buddhism, which states that suffering, Dukkha, arises from Tanha. Tanha might be thought of as improper desire, a clinging kind of love.

**Jerry:** To me, God used the word "clinging." I noticed that in one of the quotes you cited. Clinging to things, you are bound to suffer for the reason you gave earlier, Richard, that you are not self-sufficient. The things you are clinging to are not self-sufficient, as the Buddha points out dramatically. You are grabbing at lifelines, like grabbing at a rope, but nothing anchors the rope at the other end. These are false things to try to live your life by.

**Richard:** Yes, and each of the various religions has its vocabulary for entering into the ultimate state. Nirvana in Buddhism, Moksha in Hinduism, eternal life in Christianity. We might see them all as variations on the same theme. They all involve a sacrifice, a surrender of egoic self-love, so as to open oneself up to a of love of all.

**Jerry:** Yes. A key thing for giving up attachment, that clinging you are talking about, which is often called attachment, where you grasp things around you, try to hold them, and possess them. God says something to the effect of non-attachment—giving up that clinging—puts you on the right side of the great line. So you are going to be on the wrong side of the great line, which is attached to the things of the world, or on the right side of the great line, which is attached to the divine.

**Richard:** Yes, that quote is on page 202. God says,

> "**What detachment does is to put you on My side of the great line (the great divide). There is a physical reality and you can identify with that, and there is a divine reality and you can identify with that—if you detach from things first. You cannot**

**do your full work in conjunction with me without detachment."**

Of course, this is a major theme of Eastern religion, but we see it in the West as well. The religious figure in the West who best expresses the idea of living a sacrificial life so as to be wholly open to the divine is Jesus.

**Jerry:** Yes. I early on asked, "Is Jesus divine?"

**"Yes."**
"Well, divine in the sense we are all kind of divine, or some unique way?"
I am told **"in some unique way."**

Well, what way is that? It is strange because, in one sense, everything in the world is divine as part of the divine reality, but at the same time, we realize divinity in ourselves to various degrees at various moments. Most of us are low in our degree of realization of the divine aspect of our nature. Jesus was 100% full of the divine. That enabled him to provide us with the model of a finite creature capable of something like infinite love, love which knows no bounds. In one sense, that is what it is all about- how to produce the harmony. Well, love is virtually the word for harmony. If you had to sum it up in one word, it would be loving relations and loving connections. Loving connections are going to fit well together and be respectful. Jesus is also described as a way of connecting to God being completely filled, being accessible to us in a more comfortable way than the hidden invisible God who is usually hard for people to relate to. Jesus was a real person in the world, and we have the stories and his teachings, so it is easier for us to connect to Jesus. Since Jesus is a 100% divine, it is what logicians call a transitive relationship; it goes straight through. To connect to Jesus is to connect to God.

**Richard:** He is, in his own person, a revelation of what we are all striving to become. It says on page 248,

> **"He is the pure embodiment of love, a great resource and a treasure for mankind, for all who believe in him."**

He reveals the path to communion with God. As it says in the Gospel of John, he is 'the Way.' But the aim is not to worship Jesus, or to somehow get from him a ticket to heaven, but to become Jesus-like ourselves.

**Jerry:** God says heaven as a reward is like a Club Med in the sky and says, "Give Me a break!" How can that be noble and ideal? It is just as material in your afterlife as if it were your next summer vacation.

**Richard:** The goal is to live a sanctified life in this world. The ego is not to be done away with but sanctified. It needs to be brought into an awareness of its connection to the whole and into a recognition and affirmation of the good of the whole. One way we are able to do this, according to the book, is to realize that, as much as we may be struggling now, the 'victory' is already here.

**Jerry:** The Kingdom of Heaven, the Kingdom of God is already here.

**Richard:** The struggle is now, and the victory is now.

**Jerry:** Yes. The victory depends on the struggle; even though the victory from a certain time perspective has already been achieved. The victory is present and is accessible to us.

**Richard:** On page 333, God says the struggle is happening right now, yesterday's and tomorrow's struggles are happening right now—and the final victory is happening right now.

> You say, "The Kingdom of God is here now?"
> God says, "**Exactly.**"
> You say, "Is there some way for us to get in touch with that 'final victory' level or dimension?"
> God says, "**Yes! That is also Me. You access it through Me.**"

This reminded me of the first chapter of Genesis, where for six days God works to produce the creation and then rests on the seventh day. That seventh day is the victory level, which in the Jewish religion is considered holy. You are not allowed to work on the Sabbath because—to put it in the language of your book—the Sabbath is the day when you are to rest in the victory level. The rest of the week is for work, but on the Sabbath, you abide in the victory level. And that helps to give the six days of work their meaning and holiness.

This also gets expressed on page 333. You say,

> "Is it important that we relate to the level of being (if that is the right way to put it) on which the final victory occurs? Does our relating to the victory level contribute somehow to 'winning the struggle'?"
> And God says, "**Yes, oddly enough, the victory is now and the struggle is now, and yet the victory depends on the 'outcome' of the struggle.**"

**Jerry:** It sounds like a confusion about time, but since there are two time dimensions, it makes perfect sense. It makes perfect sense that we have to work with all our heart and effort to bring about the victory level with this kind of harmony and love we have been discussing. At the same time, we have already achieved it. We collectively, including the divine, have achieved it. We have already achieved it if viewed in a certain way, and we can connect with that.

## THE ESSENTIAL PROJECT OF THE DIVINE

**Richard:** And both of these dimensions of time are important, the temporal and the eternal. In fact, they complement one another. One of the criticisms of mysticism we get in the book is of the inclination of the mystic to want to meld into the divine in such a way as to no longer have to engage in the struggles of life. God clearly says, no, that is not the way. But on the other hand, we don't want to become so immersed in the struggle that we lose the inner peace of knowing that, on some level, the struggle has already been won. We need them both.

**Jerry:** Yes, that is a good premise for discussing the implications for living one's life.

**Richard:** Perhaps, then, we will pick it up from here next time and discuss how we can apply what we learn from the book. What is the takeaway? Thank you, Jerry.

**Jerry:** Very good. Well, thank you, Richard. Bless you.

# 11. The Takeaway

**Dr. Jerry L. Martin** We continue our dialogues about *God: An Autobiography*. What is the agenda for today? Where do we begin?

**Dr. Richard Oxenberg** Our plan for today is to sum things up and think about the book's takeaway. What is the book's ultimate or primary message for us? As you've mentioned, the book does not present itself as a systematic theology.

**Jerry:** That's right. God uses the term revelation. I hesitated to use that term myself, although I do believe it is God speaking to me with a message for our times. Revelation usually is taken to mean the founding book of a religion. This is not a religion being founded.

**Richard:** It is not a religion being founded. Nor is it presented as a systematic theology.

**Jerry:** That is true too. A friend of mine, when I first described the book to him, said it is a revelation about revelations. I thought he really got it right there. And you are right; it is not a kind of systematic metaphysics. You found a metaphysics underlying it, I believe, but it is not laid out as a theology.

**Richard:** Even though it is not presented as a systematic theology, it certainly has theological implications. In many ways what we have been exploring in our talks together are the theological implications of the book. I thought today we might try to summarize these theological implications—although I imagine that different people reading the book might come to different theological conclusions about it, just as people come to different theological conclusions about the Bible.

**Jerry:** Yes. What we have been doing is very much like biblical theology. You take a text that you think has some standing, in this case, because I am saying God told me this, and you try to think of what big picture one gets out of this report about the most fundamental issues—about us, God, the universe, and life. Biblical theologians go and pick texts they take to be most salient and put them together coherently. They always necessarily move beyond the text because that is the job of biblical theology. It is not just to say there is this, that, and the other thing- a basket of verses. There are certain fundamental themes that emerge, and that is what you and I have been exploring in these dialogues.

**Richard:** I have pulled out what I take to be five different theological points that the book as a whole seems to be making. One of the reasons I personally have been fascinated with the book is that in many ways it reflects theological ideas that I had already been thinking about before I ever encountered the book. Not in every way, but in many.

**Jerry:** I have been struck by that because I know some of your own thinking as you have done a careful reading of *God: An Autobiography*, you have found an amazing number of passages that you could have written.

## THE TAKEAWAY

**Richard:** Yes, the book often reflects my own thought—although it adds something as well.

**Jerry:** You pull out the verses over and over of these points about wholes and parts. It is a kind of metaphysical thinking that is not ungrounded in the text. It is right there in the text.

**Richard:** In this regard, I'll tell you a story of an experience I had in relation to my understanding of the Cross of Christ. As you know, I grew up in a Jewish family. When Jews look at the image of Jesus hanging on the cross, I think they find it rather disturbing and frightening. That was my experience upon first seeing a crucifix as a kid. I was very disturbed by the image. I asked myself: Why is this guy being tortured on this Cross, and how could anyone take solace in looking at it? My discomfort only got worse when I learned a bit about the theology behind it. Jesus was being tortured on the Cross as a substitute for us! In other words, what God is saying through the Cross is: *This is what I would do to you!* You can thank your lucky stars that I'm doing it to him instead of you—isn't that nice of me—but if I didn't have him to do it to, I'd do it to you. It's what you deserve!

I was horrified by that message. I didn't think of myself as a perfect person but I couldn't quite see how I deserved to be crucified!

But then, one day many years later, after having thought more about the underlying message of Christianity, I found myself looking at a crucifix again, in a Catholic church I was visiting. Suddenly the meaning of it shifted in my mind. It went from: *This is what I would do **to** you*, to, *this is what I would do **for** you*. In other words, Jesus' crucifixion was a sacrificial act of love. I imagine this is the way most Christians are brought up to look at it. God gave His only begotten Son out of love for the world.

This certainly seemed a better way of looking at it, but the theology still troubled me. Why was it necessary for *anyone* to suffer such torture and torment, even as an act of love?

But then, sometime later, I had another little epiphany in relation to the meaning of the Cross. It went from: *This is what I would do **for** you*, to, *this is what I am doing **with** you*. In other words, the message is that God, as immanent in the creation, goes through all the pain, hardship, and suffering of existence with us. Such problems are inherent to the nature of existence itself. God didn't create them deliberately; God suffers them with us, and through living the sacrificial life revealed by Christ, we can be conducted beyond them. That is the message of the Cross.

I came to think of this as the *participatory nature of God*. God is a full participant in the creation, not only in the good parts but in all the suffering, anguish, and problems as well. And we can take solace in knowing that we are not alone in our suffering, and that suffering will not have the final word, because God is ever with us, even in our darkest moments. And this is fully expressed in your book.

**Jerry:** Yes, it is a repeated theme. God says at one point, otherwise (if I did not suffer along with people), I would have stepped back and been a cruel observer. Look at all these people's sufferings not affecting Me, because I am eternal, unchanging, perfect. Well, that is certainly not the message of *God: An Autobiography*. God is in the thick and thin of everything right with us.

**Richard:** I think one of the things that turns people off to traditional religion is precisely that image of God as a cruel observer, who has the power to make everything better but, for some unfathomable reason, just chooses not to. That comes to be called 'the problem of evil' in theology. If God is all good and all-powerful, why does God allow all the evil in the world? Your book presents an answer to that question, which is that suffering is inherent to the nature of what-is.

**Jerry:** It is the nature of the universe, the nature of real life, and the nature of being real. The real must be material, and therefore, you might say imperfect, subject to decline and entropy. As we develop into sentient biological beings, sentience invites suffering. That is how it is. God is alive and is not just a kind of divine mental computer up there. God suffers the same way. Part of the backdrop to *God: An Autobiography*, is that we are both the same as and different from God. God is right here in us. It is not that God is just sympathizing from afar. God is right here in us, going through it.

**Richard:** Our going through it *is* God's going through it. This is a rather new way of thinking about God, at least compared to traditional ways. It's not that God sat up on some architectural throne at the beginning of time and said to Godself, "Hmm...Should I create a universe with suffering or without it?" And then said, "Well, I guess I'll make one with suffering." Rather, suffering is inherent to the nature of reality. Even God is subject to it. It presents various problems, and these problems have to be addressed, and we are called to participate in addressing these problems with God.

**Jerry:** God is a being whose role and nature is to create a world or worlds and to work with human beings in those contexts to actualize the divine nature and the world's multiplicity of values that a real-world now makes possible.

**Richard:** Yes, just as God doesn't decide that there will be suffering as opposed to no suffering, God also doesn't decide to create as opposed to not create. The creation emerges out of God with a kind of necessity. And the creation presents problems. So the problems are unavoidable. This is what I mean when I say that the creation presents problems that then have to be addressed—by God *and* us.

**Jerry:** Yes. It is automatic, you might say. It is just what God does. Once you create, you have all the specific problems of a real world. We are all in it together.

**Richard:** We are all in it together. And this, for me anyway, does a pretty nice job of resolving the traditional problem of evil. I think many people say to themselves: Well, either I have to accept the traditional idea of God, who seems to be a cruel observer, to use your phrase, or I have to reject religion altogether. The book presents us with a third way—something of a Hegelian *aufheben*.

**Jerry:** Yes. That seems like the either / or, like dialectical *aufheben*. Essentially it rises up above.

**Richard:** It rises up above the dilemma in a way that reconciles the conflicting ideas. In this case, the conflict is between the suffering in the world and the idea of the love of God. It seems we have to either deny the suffering or deny God's love. But your book presents a third alternative. Yes, there is suffering in the world, but that does not mean God is unloving or that the world is futile or meaningless. In fact, *the suffering lends meaning to the world.*

**Jerry:** It is the opposite of meaningless. Suffering, or dealing with it is what the meaning of the world is, you might say.

**Richard:** You can't quite call it pantheism; you can't quite call it panentheism. We don't have a theological word for it. I would say, '*participationism.*' There is a divine reality that we all participate in with God, and we must interact with God to resolve the problems inherent to creation.

**Jerry:** God is a person, and the personal is interpersonal. I cannot be a person, and nobody can be a person all alone. The personal is interpersonal. A little neonate discovers how to be a person by interacting with parents and then later other children. It is all interactive.

**Richard:** So that's point one. Let's call it the participatory nature of God.

## THE TAKEAWAY

Another point I pull out from the book is its presentation of *reality as teleological*. The universe is teleological in its very nature, everything is striving for fulfillment. Modern mechanistic materialism is rejected. Even God, and the God beyond God, are striving for fulfillment. The God beyond God creates in order to fulfill itself. And every moment of creation has its own teleological character.

**Jerry:** That is a very interesting implication, Richard. It is not just in some big way the world is teleological, but all the way down to you and me, and the molecules, and at every moment. That is very arresting because that is how we live life- moment to moment. Each moment has a kind of teleological thrust. A lot of the trick of life is to be in tune with that properly, managing that teleological thrust, not squelching or perverting it.

**Richard:** Our tendency to interpret the world mechanistically—which is the tendency of the modern mind due to the scientific revolution—is mistaken. And, when we reflect upon it, it makes sense that it's mistaken. If the world is mechanistic at base, then where did our teleological nature come from, our desires and aspirations? It's hard to see how these could have arisen from a strictly mechanistic universe.

**Jerry:** That is a very powerful interpretation. I read a blog by someone who likes to call us (referring to humans as) "wet robots." I do not feel like a wet robot. I have goals, I am making decisions; I have experiences that the robot does not have, wet or not wet.

**Richard:** Yes, wetness doesn't quite capture the idea of teleology.

**Jerry:** No. That is that person's attempt to conceive that we are organic, so organic is just a wet robot, but of course, that is no account at all of what life is.

**Richard:** If we begin with a mechanistic conception of the universe, how can we help but fail to understand ourselves, given that we are teleological beings? And that failure is going to impede our attempts to address the problems of life and the world. The book provides a counter conception. Here is a quote from page 166:

> **"Even on the level of physics, it is love that holds the world together, and provides its energy."**

The implication of speaking of 'love' here, is that, although we do not experience the physical forces of the world as having a subjective dimension or a subjective drive, nevertheless there is some kind of subjective drive animating them; it is not just mechanical.

**Jerry:** It is what some thinkers have called an 'inside.' We see everything from the outside just as we see one another from the outside. We can talk to one another, and learn each other's insides, but we do not talk with these elements, though they have a kind of inside, a kind of interior thrust of their own. They are not just billiard balls being banged around the table. They are actually doing something, moving forward.

**Richard:** Some quantum physicists have suggested that this is how it must be. David Bohm, I believe, proposed something along these lines.

**Jerry:** Recently, philosopher Thomas Nagel's book *Mind and Cosmos* says it is clear that there is also mind, and physics leaves that out. A mechanistic nature cannot be an adequate metaphysics, cannot write a philosophical story, or be the whole understanding of reality. He is saying we have to go back and work some more. He does not know exactly how to fill that out. He is not a religious person, but he says there is more to the story, folks.

**Richard:** There is so much more to be understood from a metaphysical point of view. One of the reasons we have trouble with this may be that our minds are not well equipped for cognizing the subjective. As Kant points out, our minds are ordered to understand the world through certain categories, such as causality and substance. But these categories are not adequate to an understanding of the subjective. Perhaps our minds will have to evolve beyond where they are now for us to be able to truly understand. God, at some point, says man may not be the ultimate end of evolution.

**Jerry:** What we cannot do now, perhaps we can do ten years from now. Telepathy, and who-knows-what?

**Richard:** Ten years from now, or ten million years from now. So, there is a general teleology—at the molecular level, at the personal level, at the interpersonal level, and at the societal level. That teleological thrust gets expressed in a passage on page 312 that I keep coming back to because it expresses something fundamental:

> God says, "**This is the ultimate story, the meaning of it all. I have a project to complete… It is in the nature of reality that the world, the totality of worlds plus Me, is here for a purpose. There is a goal.**"

You ask, "What is the goal?"

> God says, "**The goal is completeness, connectedness, to create the many and to pull them back into the one.**"

This gives us a vision of the grand teleological thrust of being. First, we have the unactualized potentiality of the God beyond God, which is a kind of oneness, but amorphous and undeveloped. Out of this oneness arises the great diversity of the world, of the many worlds. And this diversity is teleologically driven, not to go back into the undifferentiated oneness, but to make of itself a harmony. The diversity is teleologically driven toward unity, but not a unity that will eclipse separateness and individuality, but a unity that fulfills them through harmonious relations, which we might call love.

**Jerry:** Yes. Which we could call love. It has a lot of practical dimensions. Hallmark cards do not answer all your questions, but love is a good aspect. Ask, what is driving this? What is the motivation for pursuing a teleological purpose? It is to tap into your loving nature. God says, "Remember, love is what actualizes a thing." It is what makes it real and full, including God. God loves us. We love God. That brings us both to our fullest being.

**Richard:** And this has societal implications. We might say—although there is not a lot of discussion about this in the book—that the way to actualize love societally is through justice. The truly just person cares about others and not just him or herself. So, the pursuit of justice is itself an expression of love and of the desire for a loving society. This implies that the teleology of the universe has ethical implications, implications inherent to the nature of being itself. It is not just a matter of God issuing commands.

**Jerry:** Yes. That is what fulfills the divine nature, our nature, and the world's nature.

**Richard:** Another dimension of the book is its discussion of what impedes this. There seems to be something about the creation of individual beings that gives rise to selfishness. The creation itself brings with it a problem that then needs to be resolved.

**Jerry:** We enter a world of desire. That is what it is to be born into the world. You are born as an individual, as we were saying, and you are very much guided by your desires. Part of the challenge of love is to have those desires go beyond one's preoccupation with just one's own self-aggrandizement.

**Richard:** This gets expressed in the book in terms of the development of the ego. How would you express that?

**Jerry:** When I ask about the ego, God distinguishes between ego in the normal sense, which is a function of personality (we all need a good, healthy ego), and ego described as aggressive and defiant of God's will. You need self-respect. You need to be able to stand up for yourself. But there is also plundering others. It is likened, in that exchange, to cancer. Cancer is a cell that cares only about itself. Of all the cells that function organically in the whole body, the cancerous cell decides- I should take over everything. Then, of course, the cancer kills the body, so it is not a successful strategy, in the long run, even for cancer. The organic analogies, I think, are very apt here. Since God is a living being, and we are living beings, a lot of evil can be understood in these organic analogies. It is as though one of our organs is not doing its job.

Our world of multiplicity is also a world of complexity. Our bodies are examples of tremendous complexity. Complexity within a unity that is functional and achieving our teleological goals gives us a healthy life that sustains all of our systems, including our brains, mentality, moral systems, and interpersonal systems. It is always very sad when, with an organic disorder as with late-life problems or illnesses, people's personalities change and they become, say, mean. It is a kind person who is now not in command of themselves and turns mean. Well, these are the perversities that can happen. Often, of course, the worst is not when it happens in the sad case of an organic malfunction causing a personality change but when a person willfully insists on being bad, and a malevolent impulse is a possibility for each human being, and that can come to shape their entire character and desire system.

**Richard:** There are a couple of quotes that might be interesting to bring up here in relation to this. On page 53 we read,

> **"Ego is destructive, separatist, defiant of My will, self-satisfied and self-lustful."**

The separatist ego is ignorant of its relation to the whole; it sees itself as completely self-contained and develops an almost warlike stance toward the rest of reality, feeling that the only way it can secure itself is by conquering everything else. That is the origin of evil.

**Jerry:** You could probably put everything under ego if you wanted to. There is the person who values spontaneity and constantly causes problems for others, not because he is trying to take over or aggrandize, but he thinks spontaneity or artistic creativity, or existential authenticity is the primary value. The values that a person is devoted to can lead them to all kinds of horrible things. Using that organic metaphor- people can be deprived of love and, therefore, want to lash back. They got fired from their job, so they want to lash back at everybody. That is not exactly aggrandizing the ego, but it is a part malfunctioning vis-a-vis the whole.

**Richard:** Yes, perhaps more broadly then, and in keeping with the participatory nature of things, we might say that when we see a person doing evil things, that evil impulse probably does not begin altogether with that person. If you grow up in a hostile environment, in a society where nobody cares about you, you are almost forced to focus on defending yourself, because the world around you isn't providing for your basic needs. Then you are going to grow up in a distorted manner, and that distortion is going to have all kinds of negative effects.

**Jerry:** But there is also an element of agency. There is a tendency to treat the person who does wrong as if that person lacks agency or it is just reactive. But you will find people growing up in identical circumstances, some going out and becoming Unabombers and others helping the Red Cross. Some wicked people do not seem to have suffered very much. Everybody has suffered, and you can impute suffering to people who do terrible things. It is a bit of a puzzle; whatever the story is, it is an issue for social psychology.

**Richard:** Here is a quote from page 180,

> "The source of evil is falsehood, not living in the truth…"

This seems related to the Eastern notion of Avidya, ignorance, or a failure to know the good. On the Western side we can see this idea in Plato, who also believed that evil is a result of a failure to know the good.

**Jerry:** Falsehood, "not living in the truth" is rather like lying, knowingly deceiving oneself and others. In addition to that source, a person making evil choices mistakes his own self-interest for the good. It is a mistake of knowledge or understanding.

**Richard:** This leads us to my next point. The purpose of religion is to bring human beings into an awareness of this greater truth. Religion is a vehicle—at least religion when it is not distorted—a vehicle for the creation of harmony, for leading individuals and society toward a harmonious life.

**Jerry:** The form that knowledge takes and the way it is characterized is different in different traditions. Often in *God: An Autobiography*, the form that the knowledge takes is *attunement*. In other words, paying attention to the divine and staying in connection with the divine. Go back to your moment to moment idea. You are not alone flailing around, but you are in tune with, and in step with the divine. That is where the harmony comes from. God does represent a teleological function for the world. God is moving forward, God is helping us move forward, and we do that best when we are in sync with the divine.

**Richard:** And the relationship between human beings and God is itself evolving. Humans come into awareness of God as they are able to, given their own limitations and cultural situations. This is what accounts for the great diversity of religions we see in the world.

**Jerry:** Their situations are diverse, and God, in coming to them in their revelational text, is coming to them in the way they can receive. That is not a fake thing, as though God is putting on a clown suit because these people believe in clowns. It is an actual sign of God that is being activated when these people have the capacity to take that in. God steps in, and God and the people develop, and God develops in that dynamic way you are describing, Richard.

**Richard:** This is expressed in a quote from page 90,

> **"I came to all peoples, but arrived in different guises. I came to the American Indians as the Great Spirit, to the Moslems as Allah, and so on. I came to the Hindus in many forms, and hence their many stories."**

If you just take this quote all by itself, you might get the impression that God is putting on masks for different people. But that's not what the book is saying. It is saying that God's self-understanding is developing along with the human understanding of God. This is one of the more fascinating aspects of the book, one that would have to be developed if we were to try to do a full theology of the book.

**Jerry:** It is not just God discovering some aspect or feature. This interaction actualizes that aspect. God discovers a capacity in the process of developing the capacity by responding to people.

**Richard:** On page 95, God says,

> "I cannot move at a pace greater than the human reactions. That is why it is important for you to tell My story, My history of interactions with humans, from My side. You will see that a development in God is really a response to, (and) conditioned by, the development of human beings and their response to me."

The *dialectical relationship* between the human being and God is really *intimate*. It sheds a whole new light on that famous line by Augustine that God is closer to me than I am to myself. The way Augustine meant that, I think, is that God is at the base of our own personal being. But, when we look at it from the standpoint of the book, the suggestion is that God's being is intimately bound up with human being. There is no development of God other than through the development of creatures who are receptive to God. That is what the book is saying.

**Jerry:** A couple of examples that come to mind, God becomes a lawgiver in relation to the people of Israel, and they tend to react. God has set norms in every culture. God is always normative, but norms do not always take the form of the Ten Commandments. In the interaction with the people of Israel, this side of God comes to the fore.

I do not know what interaction would be such that God's norms now become commandments. It might be the formation of a people as partners, or perhaps the people were looking for rules. I am not very rule-oriented, but I dealt with people in a work situation who needed rules, so I gave them rules. In China, people react to the divine as something like cosmic harmony—cosmic in the big sense, not just the universe and starry sky, but in the largest sense. God discovers from their sensitive reaction-I am cosmic harmony. And God now becomes cosmic harmony and steps into the role. Look at how Harry Truman became president. He grows in this tremendous way, having been a somewhat obscure senator and a vice president no one expected ever to be president, and now suddenly becomes a world-shaping statesman. God's development is somewhat like that. People are given a role and grow into it. Or they respond to other people's reactions and actually develop the capacities people see in them or look to them for.

**Richard:** Yes, and if you look at the Old Testament, God becomes a lawgiver in response to the injustice of human beings. God delivers the law at Mount Sinai after liberating the Hebrews from slavery. The injustice of slavery demands a law. The harmony of the universe is shattered by such injustice. The "thou shalt nots" of the Ten Commandments are issued as an expression of the teleology of love in that context.

**Jerry:** Yes, in the real world, love sometimes requires commandments.

**Richard:** So, the book presents God as evolving along with us, suffering with us but also evolving with us. And this helps us deal with what we've called the problem of evil but which might be called, even more broadly, the problem of imperfection. The universe is not a perfect place, and it requires constant effort and work on our part to bring it as close to perfection as possible. We should not say to ourselves: If there were meaning in the universe, it would be perfect, and since it is not perfect, the universe is meaningless. Rather, the book is saying that the very imperfect nature of the universe is what lends it *meaning*.

**Jerry:** There is an awful lot of religious motivation that is yearning for perfection. If you want perfection, then you have to work very hard to find it in our world or to project it onto the divine being. If you are looking for meaning, which is the more fundamental need, that does not have to be perfect. Everything I am engaged in that fills my life with purpose is not perfect. Oddly enough, imperfection sounds, by definition, like a flaw, but in fact, it is a trait or a function, not a glitch. It is what makes the world a place of purpose and meaning—precisely that the Garden of Eden came to an end.

**Richard:** And it's not that there is some grand meaning that everything else is instrumentally related to, it's that the meaning can be realized in every moment.

**Jerry:** Right here and in every moment.

**Richard:** One of the questions I found myself asking as I read through the book is: What is the morality of the book? Does the book present a specific ethic? It is not something emphasized in the book, but I finally found it in the notion of the sacrificial. There is a passage where you go through a number of different interpretations of sacrifice which God rejects. But you finally hit on one that God endorses: True sacrifice is the surrender of one's separatist, egoistic desires to what we might call the teleology of love. In other words, the ego, by its individual nature, wants what it wants for itself. In this sense, selfishness is built into the very nature of egoic life. But in order for the teleology of the universe to work itself out, we are required to subordinate—not eliminate—but subordinate our egoic demands to the demands of love. We must say to ourselves, for instance, that even though I would like to have the *whole* blueberry pie for myself, there is somebody else here who would also like some blueberry pie, and out of love for that person, I will have a little less blueberry pie so that they can have some too. That is the sacrificial. Even though there is no discussion of particular ethical questions in the book, it is saying that life should be lived under the guidance of *the principle of sacrificial love*. Does that sound right to you?

**Jerry:** Yes, exactly. I always think more particularly than these large formulations. If you look at the different religious traditions, they overlap in the kind of moral instructions they give. They are all against selfishness of this greedy, lustful kind. All the religions say that there is more to a life that has meaning. However, their particular norms vary greatly, like the Chinese harmony or the Confucian role of responsibility that includes preserving the great tradition. These are all excellent norms. None are said to be no good. They all are ways of actualizing human fulfillment and our relation to the divine. Or, as you put it, the mandate of the teleology of love. There are a many different modes of loving or ways of living out love.

**Richard:** A lot of different ways in which love can manifest. Here is a quote about love on page 166. God is speaking,

> **"Love is the basic force in the universe. I enter the world out of love. The world yearns for Me, and turns to Me, out of love. Love forms the bond between man and woman, one neighbor and another, and the orders of nature. It is love that pulls all of nature upward, and heals the soul and repairs the breaches in the world."**

So, love is the teleological force of the universe. Again, creation out of the God beyond God separates everything. That very separation creates a hunger for reunion. That hunger for reunion is the love, the *eros*, driving everything back to everything else.

One of the things that the book does not do is present its own version of the Ten Commandments. It does not tell us how we should deal with the abortion question, or homosexual marriage, or any of these great controversial issues. We have to work these out ourselves. And it is not just we who have to work these out, but God too who is working them out with us, through us, because, as we have been saying, God is developing along with us.

But the book does not leave us without any guidance whatsoever. It tells us that we have to work out these questions under the general principle of sacrificial love. And given the inherent imperfections and limitations of life, we can pretty much expect that we are going to get it wrong frequently. So, we have to be charitable toward ourselves as well.

**Jerry:** It could be that the disagreements, say over abortion, are fruitful. Each side has something going for it, and as events change, sometimes how one evaluates the particulars of a hot moral issue changes. Sometimes even technology can change valuations. Also, we should be sensitive to our use of sacrificial love, which seems exactly right. The teleology of love is very appropriate language for *God: An Autobiography*. At the same time, we realize God is working, in a particular way, through Jerry Martin or someone else. Love is going to have different definitions in different cultures and different traditions. I like all these cross-cultural comparisons. You can always emphasize the similarity, or you can emphasize the difference, because there are always shades of difference between them. In the book, there is a distinction drawn between love and compassion—of Buddhist compassion, for example. From one perspective, they are the same thing. There is certainly the part recognizing its role in the whole in a positive and helping way, and both are necessary. You need both love and compassion.

**Richard:** In the Buddhist tradition a distinction is made between metta and karuna, where karuna is compassion and metta is more generally something like goodwill, the desire that the other be well. But karuna is specifically an entry into the other's suffering. So, compassion, specifically in that context, means caring about the suffering of others.

I remember reading an interesting dialogue with the Dalai Lama in which he was talking to a Westerner about the Buddhist notion of karuna and metta. He said that when Buddhism speaks of compassion and goodwill, it always includes the idea that you should have compassion and goodwill for yourself as well as others. Sometimes in the West, there is a notion that to be truly good you must give up on any concern for yourself. But that is not the Buddhist idea.

**Jerry:** That is a very good point. For some discussions, we have to use love in a large sense, not affixed to a very specific cultural or traditional religious traditions' understanding of love. On the other hand, some traditions may have a particular conception that is really right. That is also possible. Different traditions might emphasize different aspects or types of love. To the extent the religions specialize, what does it mean? Each may get certain things more right than the others, giving priority to them, specializing in that compassion, for example. There are ways of understanding and relating the norms in one tradition to the norms in another and understanding a plurality of norms all as valid.

**Richard:** But I would think we would want to avoid a radical relativism here. There are some things that fall outside the bounds of anything that could reasonably be called love. Slavery was not an institution that could reasonably be called an institution of love. One of the values of the book is that it recognizes that there can be many forms and expressions of love, and they can be quite different from one another in many ways, but this doesn't bring us to relativism, where there is no distinction between right and wrong, good and evil, and everything is equal to everything else.

**Jerry:** One of the hardest things for people to hold on to, maybe for psychological reasons, is having *a diversity of values*. A diversity of ways of living one's life. Each of a number of ways is completely valid. There is another diversity that would not be valid.

Just because there is more than one valid way does not mean that each one cannot explain why it is valid or even the best way, in its own terms. It is not just a mute fact that, for some people, a certain way of life seems okay. They can understand it in their own terms, but there is another challenge: Can they explain it in human terms that people outside the tradition can understand? We all live in the same world and under the same dome of heaven. According to *God: An Autobiography*, with all of its appreciation of diversity and particularity, your life may well be different from mine. You may have a different calling than I have, for example. It is crucial that you get your calling right and that I get my calling right. They do not necessarily need to be the same calling. Yours is right for you and your situation; mine is right for me in my situation. You can generalize that up to the level of cultures as long as they are achieving values of a high order. Their values, you might say, move the universe forward, so God wants them to achieve them.

**Richard:** Another point we should probably emphasize in this context is that, as the book presents it, the human being participates in the whole universe, continuing on beyond individual life. This is not our only shot. Recognizing this also allows us to see ourselves as part of the grander whole. We are not isolated in our individual lives.

So, in terms of the general takeaway we get from the book, one of the words that comes to mind is non-dogmatic. It is participatory rather than hierarchical. There is no autocratic divine authority to which human beings are answerable. Everybody—including God—is trying to work it out together.

**Jerry:** The main reason for the lack of dogmatism is that there are multiple truths. In this world, there is a vertical dimension. There is a difference between up and down, right and wrong, truth and falsity. That is not something to be formulated in propositions, in a set of theological creeds, for example. It is not to be formulated in that way. It is too dynamic for that, too diverse, too particularistic, because it varies from person to person, from situation to situation, from culture and age to culture and age. Nevertheless, in each of those, there is a vertical dimension and a right and a wrong or a better and worse, and that unfolds.

**Richard:** And though the book is a revelation, it is not intended to found a new religion.

**Jerry:** In a way, there is nothing new here about the divine or the ultimate reality.

**Richard:** In a way, there is and isn't something new. There's a lot new, but the book is not trying to start a new religion but a new orientation to religion. Here is a significant quote from page 44. God says,

> "Now we need a new systematic revelation, from bottom to top, almost to start over again—with a (new) Genesis, one might say, with a new gospel of John. And a new philosophical understanding of God. The old one was only partly inspired and contains too much of the arrogance of human reason. Mankind does not live in a period for a Great Prophet. There can be no new Moses or other Deliverer. There can at best be Elijahs—prophets and seers—people who explain My story in a form that can be understood by this age."

That is what this book is a contribution to.

**Jerry:** That is what it is, yes, exactly. It is for people to take this divine communication in and, in light of it, move forward because it is a process.

# THE TAKEAWAY

**Richard:** One of the ways you are taking it forward is through the *Theology Without Walls* project. How is that related to all of this?

**Jerry:** Toward the very end of the book, in light of what God had told me about the revelations to the different cultures, in the wake of that, I was told to start a new theological project which struck me as virtually impossible. For one thing, I am a philosopher not a theologian, and I did not even know any theologians. I had to learn more about religion, so I started attending American Academy of Religion meetings- the official organization of all theologians and religious studies scholars. I made a point of getting to know some members and speaking to them one-on-one.

One week before the Baltimore meeting, whatever year that was, I was told it was time to start it. I printed out some of what I have been told in prayer and made some notes. I had given one talk that is reported in the book about Theology Without Walls and found most people were responsive. We proposed a panel to the most natural group, the comparative theology group. They turned it down. But I found you can schedule your own panel for a very modest fee, so we did that. I did not know if anybody would come. Nobody had heard of Jerry Martin or Theology Without Walls. We did have some distinguished panelists who had become interested from my talking with them, and I asked them to let everybody on their email list know because I was afraid nobody would come. As it turned out, it was standing room only! I thought, this is amazing. There were people literally standing in the doorway the whole time, craning their necks to hear what was being said.

**Richard:** There is a hunger for this message.

**Jerry:** There is a hunger for it. As soon as I looked around and saw what was happening to religion, I saw that these days, scholars do not study only their own tradition, they study other religions as well. The first people doing this were missionaries. They often reported that these other peoples are already very spiritual. At first, their beliefs looked superstitious since they worshipped gods portrayed in unfamiliar ways. The Hindus have a God with an elephant's head, for example. That kind of iconography is off-putting to an alien culture. But, as they started getting to know the other religions, they found their scriptures to be profound, and the people to be holy. You know, people are supposed to be holy, and they are holy. They have this deep, deep spiritual life, and you can multiply that across the cultures.

One person I got to know is Kenneth Cracknell, who is a pioneer in Interfaith Dialogue. At first he was a young Methodist charged up to spread the word, going off to the Igbo tribe in western Africa. To his amazement, he said the Igbo already knew a lot about God, and they learned from him, but he also learned from them. This sort of understanding started developing and now scholars do it routinely. Divinity schools do it routinely. They have courses in the theology of religions, asking within one's own tradition, what to make of the fact there are other religions. Do they have any saving truth, or how do they relate to what my church teaches?

In light of this broader understanding and appreciation of multiple religions, a new phase of theology seemed inevitable. I started almost every talk with what I just called The Syllogism, which was both simple and definitive: if the aim of theology is to know all we can about the divine or ultimate reality, and if there are revelations, enlightenments, epiphanies, and insights about that reality in more than one tradition, then theology can't just be what they call confessional theology, cannot be just the interpretation of one's own tradition. It should be theology without those limits, hence, Theology Without Walls.

That project has flourished. We have had several sessions every year since that first one in San Diego. We have edited several special issues of religion journals. And then, sooner than I would have thought, John Thatamanil, a theologian at Union Theological Seminary, said these papers are a goldmine, we should publish a volume of essays. It is time, so to speak, to plant the flag. That is what you do in academia; you have to plant the flag by bringing out a volume. So we brought out a volume in 2019, called *Theology Without Walls: The Transreligious Imperative*. If you want to know the divine fully and want to relate to the divine more adequately, then you have to take in the multiple traditions, the many aspects of the divine. That does not mean you have to run around worshiping in multiple traditions. Even if you stay right within a tradition, you have to understand that your tradition is part of a larger story rather than start claiming exclusivity. You were a contributor to that volume. You wrote a very fine essay that is right up in the first section.

**Richard:** Of course, that there is revelatory truth to be found in all the different religions is something that has been traditionally denied in many religions. But as people become exposed to these different religions, it becomes harder and harder to deny it.

**Jerry:** Yes, if you are really studying them with an open mind, the way you are supposed to study things. So you take it in, and then, wow, these are really impressive.

**Richard:** Yes, and what we've had up until just recently in modernity is a choice between dogmatic religion and atheistic secularism. People have felt that they had to choose one or the other. But your book is telling us that this is a false dichotomy. There is a spiritual dimension to life, it is *nondogmatic*, it is part of the human telos to pursue it, and we can be charitable toward ourselves and each other in our pursuit of it.

**Jerry:** Yes, exactly. We will stop on that very positive note. Thank you, Richard, for the wonderful set of dialogues we are having.

# 12. Conclusion: How to Live

**Dr. Richard Oxenberg** Throughout our dialogues, we have been discussing the big theological vision presented by the book. Today, our focus is on how that theological vision may affect the way people live their lives.

**Dr. Jerry L. Martin** I thought in the last dialogue, Richard, you gave a beautiful account, a kind of synopsis of the basic vision of *God: An Autobiography*, of God coming into the world, splintering in all different directions, and then working to bring it all together again.

**Richard:** Perhaps the most distinctive practical implication of the book, is how it would affect—were it generally accepted—the way religious people think about themselves and their relationship to other religions.

The theologian Alan Race came up with a threefold classification of religious attitudes toward other religions, which he called exclusivism, inclusivism, and pluralism. Exclusivism is the view that one's own religion is correct and all the others false. Inclusivism is the view that all the religions are saying the same thing and therefore can be rolled up into one universal religion. Pluralism is the view that, though the religions are truly different, they all reflect some dimension of the truth.

But I think your book suggests a fourth way of looking at this, which we might call *complementalism*—this is the view that the different religions, though truly different from one another, nevertheless complement one another. Each religion may be viewed as a piece of a bigger puzzle, such that, when you put them all together, you get something more complete than when you look at each one separately. This suggests that the religions can learn from one another.

This would not only be a new way of looking at religion from a theological point of view, but also from the point of view of religious practice. It implies that people can benefit from participating in the practices of other religions.

There is a quote toward the end of the book that expresses this, on page 358,

> **"You stand on the threshold of a new spiritual era, a new axial age, in which, for the first time, spiritually attuned individuals will draw their understanding of spiritual reality, not just from scriptures of their own religious tradition, but from the plenitude of My communications to men and women."**

If that idea were to gain currency among the different religions, it would radically change how the religions relate to one another and understand themselves. It would also change the way religious people pursue spirituality.

**Jerry:** God told me that the division of labor can continue. In other words, those in each religion can continue to do their thing, to worship in their own way, to preserve their own heritage. In *God: An Autobiography*, God is a multiplex being with many aspects and dimensions. It would have been overwhelming for a single culture to have tried to develop the whole, complex truth from the beginning, but understandings have developed in various cultures and today we can all study them.

We can take in many spiritual fruits and, at the same time, continue our paths in spiritual orientation, but now understanding that our own tradition is not the whole story. It is not the only path. It is not the only set of truths. There are many truths. There is no reason for one set of truths to contradict another set of truths, even though they are different- different vocabularies, different aspects of the divine, and different aspects of human life.

**Richard:** From a practical point of view, the average Western person going to church or synagogue with this understanding would now be open to learning and deepening their spirituality through, say, Buddhism and Hinduism. Judaism could open itself to truths expressed in the gospels, Christianity could open itself to the Talmud, and each could be enriched by the other.

**Jerry:** Yes, exactly. They can do it as a serious study of each other or in a more casual way. Some churches already bring in lecturers on different religions—in part to be citizens of the world in the 21st century. From the different religions, we can trade insights. I first imagined something like a big swap-meet. We all get together, and I see your truths, you see my truths, and we trade. We all walk away from the swap-meet happy and more enlightened, having a bigger share of spiritual insights.

However, God tells me, "No. It is not just that; this will be a dynamic process." Once you understand the truths in other traditions, that affects your own thinking. Even if you are in your traditional worship and do what you have always done, you will be doing it in a new way and with a new understanding. At a thinking level, you will be expanding, and it will be dynamic. You may think, "Well, I agree with that, but I do not agree with that," as you filter it through.

For example, you can translate the Bhagavad Gita, action without attachment to results, into Christian terms. You may understand the Christian or Jewish traditions differently after you take in the Bhagavad Gita. After taking in Christian and Jewish traditions, the Hindu may be affected and read the Bhagavad Gita in a different way. It will be a dynamic process.

**Richard:** Yes, and this approach to religion reinforces the basic religious teachings of Christianity and Judaism of loving your neighbor as yourself.

We live in a global world where everybody on Earth is our neighbor. To believe that only your religion is correct, and all the others dangerously in error, is to live with a sense of suspicion and threat. If one were to embrace this new approach, then that would drop away. Not only would religions dialogue with one another in order to understand one another better, but they would dialogue with one another to better understand themselves.

**Jerry:** And to get a better understanding of reality.

**Richard:** And to get a better understanding of reality.

One of my favorite passages in the book is where you and God are talking about the importance of individual personhood, how the ultimate goal of spirituality is not to merge into some amorphous impersonal Absolute, as is sometimes suggested in mystical traditions.

> You say to God, "So, mysticism is precisely wrong, backward."
> And God responds, **"Don't get carried away."**

Don't get carried away because there is something to be learned from the mystical notion of Unity and the mystical experience of Oneness. We can bring that experience back into the world of diversity and live in closer communion with one another and with God, having recognized the ultimate unity underlying the multiplicity.

**Jerry:** Yes. In our unity with the divine, the God in us, and we in God, applies to our neighbor as well, including our neighbor halfway around the world.

When Abigail and I visited India, they bowed towards us with prayerful hands and said, "Namaste." It was explained to me that this means, "The God in me greets the God in you." I thought that, even with your bitterest enemy, you could say that because it is not the God in them that you object to. Often, they are not living up to the God within themselves. That's what you object to.

**Richard:** And that is implicit in the notion that runs through the entire book concerning the unity—or what we might call the dialectic—of self and other.

On one level, we are different from one another, and on another level, we are ontologically united with one another, and we need to hold both these truths in our minds in order for us to relate to one another properly.

**Jerry:** Our actions then would manifest that.

**Richard:** If the average religious devotee were to embrace this notion, we would move from a dogmatic approach to religion to a dialectical approach to religion.

**Jerry:** Yes, dialectical. It is almost dialogical- a creative process where the ideas that are not identical and are differentiated are in a productive tension or development with each other. This dialogical aspect leads to something higher than where you started.

**Richard:** You do not simply insist upon your own point of view as the only truth but recognize that even an opposing point of view may enrich your own.

**Jerry:** It opens up possibilities that your viewpoint may have yet to consider. It is not so much alien or contradictory to your point of view as it opens a whole new dimension.

I remember the Harvard scholar Diana Eck's book, *From Bozeman to Banaras*, about her childhood as a Methodist in a Methodist town, later traveling to the holy city in India. She notices with surprise that the priests come and play with God, and they bring toys. Once you get into the Hindu tradition, this is Krishna, a God with many stories from boyhood, and he was a prankster as a boy.

We have very little about this in the Christian tradition, with very little about the childhood of Jesus. Presumably, Jesus would be a child and play and get into childish mischief, but this is completely outside the way Christians think about Jesus. Whether it is a good thing is not for me to say, but each person can take it in and see for themselves.

**Richard:** Well, we can find something of a parallel in Western religion. Jesus says, "Suffer the little children to come unto me for such is the kingdom of heaven." There is a holy dimension to the joyous innocence, and maybe even the joyous prankishness, we see in little children, which may be what the Hindu priests are celebrating in playing with Krishna.

**Jerry:** It opens one up to focus on something. All well-read, well-versed Christians would know those passages, yet they may never have focused on the implications for children or for being a child.

**Richard:** By looking at the different religions as complementary, we may come to see elements in other religions that highlight elements in our own religion that tend to be underemphasized—such as, in this case, the holiness of the childlike spirit.

## CONCLUSION: HOW TO LIVE

**Jerry:** This example is exactly what comparative theology does. I am thinking of the work of Francis Clooney, who reads for example, a Hindu goddess in parallel with some of the major texts of the tradition venerating Mary, mother of God. Mary is not a goddess; that is one of the differences. Nevertheless, Mary has a halo, so Clooney explores what one can learn from this comparison. Most religions do have a feminine Divine. Christianity gets that in through the mother of God. It invites us to explore the resonances and implication of Jesus having this devoted mother.

**Richard:** Yes. In Judaism, we have the Shechinah, which is also feminine.

This approach would lead us to replace doctrines of infallibility—the notion that revelation is infallible—with a doctrine of what we might call *creative fallibilism*. At one point in the book God says to you that you are a fallible receptor.

**Jerry:** Yes. There is nothing infallible here. I am not given any authority to say this is the one true word. No. I ask God, "What is my role?" God tells me simply "to be a serious reporter of what you are told when you pray." Period. No claim to infallibility and no mandate to found a religion. Human beings are fallible instruments in every revelation to a human being. This does not prevent them from being revelations from the divine.

**Richard:** We can extend this to all revelation, whether the Hebrew Bible, the New Testament, the Koran, or the Hindu Vedas. Whatever is regarded as revelatory should also be recognized as fallible.

And this fallibility exists in two dimensions. One is that the receivers of revelation are fallible receptors, as you say. And the other is that—at least as the book presents it—even God is fallible.

**Jerry:** I do not focus on that—the possibility of divine fallibility—but God is evolving.

**Richard:** God says in a number of places in the book, "Well, I was young then. I did not fully understand things then. I have learned something since then." That is so different from how we traditionally think of God. And this has practical implications for the way we approach moral questions in relation to religion: the question of abortion, or LGBTQ rights, for instance. We can't simply turn to a revelatory text to tell us what to do. We have to wrestle with the issues ourselves, in partnership with God, but not in blind submission to some revelation of old.

**Jerry:** Yes. We are partners.

**Richard:** God is not sitting up high with all the answers. God is getting at the truth through *our* struggle to get at the truth. We are discovering them together.

**Jerry:** Yes. I always think of the moment God said to Abraham, "Go sacrifice your son." He got up the next morning and headed for the mountain.

But, at a later moment, when it comes to Sodom and Gomorrah, the same Abraham of total obedience says, "Wait a minute, what if there are righteous men there? Are we going to destroy the whole city?" He argues with God and, as I take it, says, "Live up to your job description, God. You are supposed to be just."

God gives in and says, "If there are ten righteous men, I will save it." God learned something from that exchange about providing justice and being an exemplar of justice.

**Richard:** Yes, God is discovering Godself through our discovery of God. There is a passage in the book where God says, speaking of Hinduism, I learned that I had an Atman through the fact that human beings learned that they have an Atman.

**Jerry:** Yes, that is right. It is as though, in some sense, God vaguely knew all along, but this is how learning is. In this case, it was through human beings giving "Atman" a name, which then became articulated as a concept in human language.

**Richard:** The implication is that when we discover something, our discovery of it *is* God's discovery of it. The human being and God are ontologically enmeshed in one another. On page 167, for instance, God says,

> "I am limited and incomplete—in a sense, not all powerful; in a sense, not all-knowing; in a sense, not all-good. I am searching for My own fullness, and since I am also the World—the totality - I - the world - mankind are all seeking fulfillment (fullness) together in partnership."

**Jerry:** This was said to me in a very early dialogue with God, and these ideas blew me away. I said to God right after that, "You just contradicted the three main attributes of God as traditionally conceived." God is not disturbed that the real divine does not conform to our ideas. Our ideas need to conform to the divine.

**Richard:** And this, again, presents us with a new way of dealing with moral questions from a religious point of view. The dogmatic way leads to enormous polarization, as we see increasingly in our society. The biblical infallibilist who is persuaded that God has spoken definitively in the Bible on some issue, such as homosexuality, doesn't have a lot of room to maneuver.

**Jerry:** They have codes of behavior that are believed to be divinely derived. What are the instruments? We are talking about how we take all these disparate parts, people, and religions and get some harmony out of them or get some kind of integration where they work together rather than at odds. So, what are the instruments of harmony or unity or of bringing things together?

What is also a major theme said over and over in the book (to the point that I object that it sounds like a Hallmark card), it is all love. All love. God says, "That about sums it up."

Love is one of the major instruments of harmony, integration, and healing. Love may tell you something about how to treat these questions. It also tells you how to treat the people who disagree with you about these questions.

I had a young woman working for me, a Catholic convert, who was extremely anti-abortion to the extent that she would go picket at clinics on weekends. She was a very fine young woman. We were sitting around a table waiting for a dinner speaker. A guy at our table, a Notre Dame graduate, was talking in great contempt about the university for not giving an award to a pro-choice politician. I thought she would jump out of her chair and lunge at him, but she said nothing. I asked afterward, "You did not say anything to that guy. Why not?"

She said, "I could not think of anything loving to say." That is good advice.

**Richard:** Or we might take this one step further and suggest that, with the new attitude suggested by your book, we *can* think of something loving to say. In other words, we can lovingly disagree and engage in loving discourse about our disagreements. We can do this in recognition that the matter is not settled. It's not as if there is an absolute answer to the abortion question imprinted somewhere in the heavens and we simply need to find it out. The abortion question is complex, something that we—together with God, and when I say together with God, I mean together with our loving impulses inspired by God—must struggle to address as best we can, recognizing the multifaceted dimensions of the issue.

## CONCLUSION: HOW TO LIVE

**Jerry:** Yes. Realizing in that context, our fallibility understood as what you were calling creative fallibilism and something like a creator form of fallibility, is *humility.*

Humility is being open to a different point of view. Even when you come to an earnest conclusion that seems sound, still, you know that it is not necessarily the final word because you are not infallible. As you point out, these issues evolve. Medical technology changes the facts on the ground that you are dealing with, so the notion of creative fallibilism, approaching these things with humility, with love, with earnest commitments, respects that the other person has other earnest commitments, and you have to take them all into account.

**Richard:** Yes, and it's helpful to recognize that our struggle with these issues in an earnest and loving way *is* God's struggle with these issues. God is figuring it out with us, as we are figuring it out with God. Such an approach opens us to a recognition of the validity of opposing points of view.

**Jerry:** Yes, that is often the case. You might consider other valid points and still come to your same earnest conclusion on the one side of a question that you begin with and consider it as being held in good faith. This approach is a corrective to the tendency not only to be dogmatic about opinions but to demonize the people who disagree with you.

We live in a peculiarly pluralistic time. A good example is vegetarianism. I am not a vegetarian. I do not feel any impulse in that direction. Nothing leads me to open that door for serious exploration. On the other hand, it is perfectly conceivable, especially as one finds alternative ways to produce tasty protein, that there will come a time when people look back on our era with shock and horror. "They knew animals suffered, and yet they ate them."

**Richard:** Somewhat like how we are shocked at the idea of animal sacrifice. If we went into a church and the priest said, okay, today we're going to sacrifice a goat, I think everybody would be a little appalled.

**Jerry:** They would all be very disturbed by that, yet that is one of the most widespread religious rituals in world culture.

**Richard:** Maybe all of this tells us why God chose to reveal the divine self to a philosopher. The book is an endorsement of the philosophic process. Struggling with these questions is what we do in philosophy. The book is very Socratic in that way.

**Jerry:** The key to Socratic wisdom is that it is not based on the claim of having already found wisdom. Philosophy is the *love* of wisdom; it is the search for wisdom. If you are searching for wisdom, that is wisdom. The wisest are those who search for wisdom.

**Richard:** You arrive at provisional conclusions. You say: this is where we've gotten so far; this is the best answer we have at the moment, but we recognize that there is still more to know and understand. We continue to examine the question, perhaps one day to arrive at an even better answer. That is the Socratic process. And the book seems to be endorsing that process.

**Jerry:** We might say the same about the historical process. What happens in the history of culture? Someone as wise as Aristotle endorsed natural slavery. He thought some people were slaves by nature. That did not have racial overtones back then, but it still would not be considered now an enlightened view.

He was a great scientist but had an absurd view of women. He says that, for most species, the genus and differentia are identical. Man is a rational animal, but the human species is unusual because females do not enact the full essence of the species. They are not rational. Well, that belief is a product of his times, but these things happen, and they happen repeatedly. One century's deep wisdom is the very thing about which the next century says, "Well, they sure got that wrong." We do not have the perspective to say what it will be, but the next century may fault our most cherished beliefs.

Of course, except when each century or generation is dogmatic, what they are doing is not actually rejecting earlier views, which is often how it feels. They are doing a dialectic. They are taking earlier ideas of wisdom into account, but coming up with a new view in light of what is valued in the latest turn of thought or cultural development. They are adding something to it because they are now in a different position.

**Richard:** We could also call the historical the evolutionary. As the book presents it, God and we are evolving toward higher truths together. There is a suggestion that we can only arrive at these higher truths *through* the process of living. You have to live, make mistakes and learn from those mistakes. In some ways, that is the adventure of the cosmos that God and we are involved in together.

**Jerry:** Yes, you have to go through that process. We do not know if we finally came up with the right set of truths or moral insights, but we do have some sense of direction that enables us to recognize the limitations of what we now think.

Maybe it will take a new generation to recognize them, but collectively and with God participating in us, we can have enough sense of direction to see that our previous beliefs were inadequate in certain ways. We could not see it before very readily, but once you have gotten to a certain point, now you can see it.

**Richard:** Another important aspect of the book with practical implications is its emphasis on the sanctity of the personal. There is a tendency to feel that because we die, because the person does not last, attachment to personhood is a mistake. We find this in the

Eastern religions more so than in the Western, that to truly commune with the divine we must give up on the idea of individual personhood; we must merge with the Absolute as a drop of water merges with the ocean. The ocean doesn't die.

**Jerry:** Yes, the personal. The book I am now writing puts forth my own views, informed of course by the God book. It is tentatively titled, *Radically Personal.* The personal is, you might say, the abiding place of the divine.

There is always a metaphysical prejudice on behalf of the permanent. What is permanent is considered more real, or real in a more fundamental sense, than what is not permanent. However, that attitude is certainly not endorsed in *God: An Autobiography.*

This book says that we do not actually die, but that is not where the key is. The meaning of life is in living. Our work with God is in this world. It is not that we are living now for some future life. We are living now to live properly this life in this world, which is what God is doing. God is not waiting for us to die so we can be assigned up or down in the afterlife. God is working with us in this world and this life.

**Richard:** One of the things that I have always appreciated about the book is the balance it provides. There is life after death, but the purpose of life is not to get there. The purpose of life, as you say, is to live it now. Still, there is great comfort in knowing that we are not confined to this one life. If we blow it in this life, that is not the end of the story.

**Jerry:** That is part of the diversity. We are diversified so far that we live multiple lives as different people. In a portrayal shown to me, in what looks like Heaven, you have a moment of overview or wisdom, and then you go into another life. There are more worlds and more work to be done, and more sides of oneself to explore and develop.

## CONCLUSION: HOW TO LIVE

If we do not get it right in this life, or even if we do a great job, there is still more to be done.

**Richard:** We need more than one life because one life does not afford us the opportunity to actualize all the potentialities striving for actualization within us and within the whole cosmos. The good news of the revelation is that we will have the opportunity to actualize all these potentialities, and this opportunity never goes away. It is an ongoing adventure, and knowing this or believing it can liberate us to focus on the present.

**Jerry:** Good point.

**Richard:** There is a passage in the Sermon on the Mount in which Jesus says, "Do not worry about tomorrow, for tomorrow will worry about itself." The book is saying something similar. We shouldn't squander our present trying to ensure our future. The future will be there, forever. And this allows us to focus on making the present the best it can be.

**Jerry:** One of the implications is that your challenge in this life is to figure out where you best relate to the divine. Maybe it will be in the church you were born into, or it may be some other that comes along. What is your role—to go back to the notion of harmony—in the whole? We have different roles, after all. There is not a single right way to live.

I have never liked the question, "What would Jesus do?" I am not Jesus, and it does not really matter what Jesus would do. Instead, I ask, what makes sense in Jerry's situation for a person like Jerry to do? Or, less generically, what should I do? What is my role, my assignment?

The key is to determine your own niche. I was telling somebody the other day the story of the tuba player in a symphony orchestra. One day, he was sick and sat in the audience. He had never heard the full orchestra before. He told his friends after it was amazing. "You know the part where I am going oompa, oompa, oompa, the rest is going Yah-Da-Da-DAH-DA"—it is the grand march from Aida. However, his job is not to go mimic the full orchestra. His playing the repetitive tuba notes is his right contribution to the whole. He is doing his part. Each of us needs to find ours.

Many of our life challenges have to do with finding our niche, but it is not quite that minimal. It sometimes starts with one's role. You are born to certain parents; you have obligations, a certain situation, historical and sociological, and are born with a certain set of talents and challenges. So, figure out what is your call? What is your calling? What should you be doing?

F. H. Bradley, the British philosopher, has a celebrated essay called *My Station and Its Duties*. Well, you start there. You are a father, you are a college professor, and you are many other things as well. You start with a station and duties, and the station can change. Sometimes you need to do something different that is your true calling. Sometimes your calling changes or varies with the circumstances. A lot of life is trying to pay attention to where you are located, who you are in relationship to, what your duties are, and what goods you can achieve in the situation.

**Richard:** This is related to the discussion in the book about dharma. Everybody has their dharma. And again, we can see how the different religions speak about similar things with different words. Hinduism speaks of dharma. In the Christian tradition, a similar idea is expressed with the word 'calling.'

We have a calling or dharma to fulfill. Responsibilities to others, but also to ourselves.

**Jerry:** You develop yourself. Among your responsibilities is some obligation to your talents and to actualize them. That is a good for you, and it is a good for the world.

## CONCLUSION: HOW TO LIVE

**Richard:** And this is related to the book's discussion of the sacrificial. On page 306, God says,

> "The motive for entering the world is itself sacrificial. We—humans and me, do not enter the world to be selfish, but to live surrendering lives, sacrificial lives."

Often, when we see the word sacrificial, we think of it as self-abnegation. But that's not the book's understanding of sacrificial. To be sacrificial, in the book, is to live in recognition of your relation to others. To use the tuba player example, if you are playing an instrument in an orchestra, your job is to harmonize with the orchestra, not just to do whatever it is you personally feel like doing. That is the sacrificial dimension—to recognize that we, together with the others with whom we are in relation, must work together toward a harmonious, unified, whole. And we achieve our own greatest fulfillment by participating and contributing to this harmonious whole.

**Jerry:** That is right. One of the problems with group activity is that you will have somebody who thinks, "I am such a good musician. I will play louder than the others." Or an actor who steals every scene, draws all the attention and wrecks the whole thing. In an organization, if you have somebody chairing the meeting, and you keep interrupting them, you may be eloquent, but it is not the time to be standing up making speeches. One of the instruments of harmony is sensitivity to other individuals. How to speak to someone when they are grieving is another social sensibility. When to speak up and when to remain silent is often challenging. You go through an inner debate sometimes. Should I speak up at this point, or will that be too abrupt or out of turn? I need to find the right moment.

At the same time, we need some conflict. Conflict is not the same as disharmony because the conflict can be the creative side we are talking about, the dialectical. That is always a question- is this a moment for challenging something and creating a moment of conflict? Maybe it is, maybe it is not, and we make those decisions daily.

**Richard:** Every moment has its opportunity—its 'calling,' so to speak. We are called to make this the best version of this particular moment.

**Jerry:** Yes, very nicely put. Each moment has deep meaning. The meaning is not at the end. A story or novel tends to be written with a view to the end, and some conceptions of life or history are that way. The meaning is at the end, but that is not how life is lived. The meaning of George Washington's life was not that last sickly year or two, for example. The end of Lincoln's life is, in a way, symbolic, but the fact that he was assassinated is not the meaning of Lincoln's life. Each of these moments, when you are going along, has its integrity as a moment and you have to live that moment in its best way.

**Richard:** Yes, but again there's a balance, a dialectic between present and future. It's not as if the present is divorced from the future. As we've said before, it is something like a football game. The purpose of playing football is not to get touchdowns; the purpose of getting touchdowns is to play football. The reason you have the touchdowns is so that you can play the game, not vice-versa. There is a goal, but the goal is for the sake of the play.

**Jerry:** It is a goal totally defined by the game. As we live, these moments, not all of which seem salient, dramatic, and interesting, have their role, like each note. Even in repetitive or quiet parts, each note has its role, and it needs to be that note. With our behavior, we always need to strike the right note.

**Richard:** One of the book's messages, and we find this in many different religions, is that we are never alone in this struggle to find the right note. God is with us, and we realize this through prayer and faith.

At one point in the book, you have an experience of union with God. You thought it felt strange, and God responds,

> **"There is nothing strange about it. That is how the universe is. The parts can communicate with the whole."**

I thought that was an interesting way of understanding prayer and faith.

In a sense, when we are praying, we are trying to commune with the greater whole of which we are a part. In doing so, we expand ourselves. Rather than see ourselves as confined to the little space we are in, we see ourselves as situated within the greater whole, the eternal whole. That can be a liberating and illuminating experience.

**Jerry:** A lot of the meaning of your life is precisely in that connection. You can connect with the whole. The whole can also connect with you. This is probably the point of many kinds of worship and meditation, a way of connecting with the whole.

A friend of mine, a serious Jewish scholar who prays, says he always wonders if anybody is listening. Part of his hesitation was— why would God care that I pray? God is so much bigger than me. How could my meagre prayer possibly be registering?

I thought, "Well, you are underestimating God, for one thing." How can the phone lines handle the trillion calls made simultaneously during the day? Well, God is like that, but bigger. Moreover, God is interested in your prayer, and your prayer is a direct connection to the whole.

**Richard:** Yes, and to recognize God as participatory is to recognize that God is right there in our prayers. Something similar is said in the New Testament, where Paul speaks of the Holy Spirit praying through him when he prays.

Yet another of the practical takeaways from the book concerns its treatment of suffering. The book has some interesting things to say about suffering. We often think of suffering as a negation of life and it can lead to a great deal of anger at God, if we imagine God to be an omnipotent being who could, if only God would, eliminate suffering with the lift of a pinky.

We get a very different understanding of suffering in the book. Suffering is integral to the nature of reality. God did not put it there; it is part of the nature of what-is. God confronts it as humans confront it. Once again, we are in it together.

**Jerry:** God suffers when we suffer because God's project in some way is to get Himself/Herself/Itself integrated. Integrated so that everything is functional rather than having these dysfunctional parts going off on their own. Our suffering is just unraveling. Just as it is unraveling our sense of ourselves and the meaning of our lives, it is unraveling God's efforts.

**Richard:** And still the book provides great hope. Suffering is inevitable but not final. We are going to get past the suffering, it is never absolute. There will always be another opportunity, no matter how awful the present moment may seem. That is an important message. Beyond that, we are told that suffering is important for growth.

**Jerry:** "Suffering is the law of growth in the universe." The analogy given to me is much like muscles. How do the muscles get stronger? They get stronger by being torn apart in exercise and then build up again. One day to tear them apart, another day for them to grow together, and then they are stronger.

Early on, I brought up my moments of suffering. God asked me to bring them up because this topic had come up, and one of the questions was- what did you learn from that? What would have been missing if you had not gone through that experience? These answers never quite satisfied me because I might have learned something from many of the experiences of suffering, once you think about it, but from every one of them?

**Richard:** I think the book gives us two messages about suffering, both of which are important for us to bear in mind. One is that suffering *can* lead to growth, and we should look to see the opportunities for growth that suffering provides. But the other is that suffering is simply part of the fabric of the universe. We cannot escape it, but mustn't be defeated by it.

**Jerry:** I am told it is the condition of the world being real. Without the world being real, you are not real. Nothing is real. A perfect world would be a hologram world where nothing is real, nothing is happening, and there are no real people. They are all hologram people. Throw us into a reality that includes the high development that involves organic beings, animals, and people. Part of that is the entropy that all physical matter suffers, but also the organic cycles of growth, maturation, sickness, death, and aging to which all living beings are subject.

You do not want to say, "Well, I would rather be a robot, and then I would not go through that process of aging and things going wrong and slowly moving toward death." That would be less fulfilling. It would be a world of radically less meaning, almost devoid of meaning, without suffering. The world with suffering is, oddly enough, full of meaning. Suffering, dealing with it, and learning from it, are central to the drama.

**Richard:** I'm reminded of the question of John Stuart Mill: "Which would be better, to be a suffering Socrates or a happy pig?" It is a richer experience to be a suffering Socrates. Socrates is strangely happier than the happy pig, even though much suffering is involved.

**Jerry:** Mill thought the pleasure principle was ultimate but, even so, he saw that Socrates has a role that leads to his conviction, and he is condemned to die from hemlock. Yet one does have the sense that through that whole process he is happy. He thinks the only thing that really matters in life is the condition of your soul. None of his suffering touched that. The fact that he was unfairly convicted does not touch his soul. That is why he says, "No ill can come to a good man," because the ill does not affect the soul. Only the person can distort their soul.

Look at the kinds of things some people choose to do. They choose to sail through storms. They join rescue parties to track people down in the mountains, in the bitter cold, with many risks. People do that, and that is not unhappiness; what counts is the kind of happiness.

**Richard:** One of the religious sayings that has always given me solace is from Julian of Norwich, the 14th century Christian anchoress. She was very distressed about the Church's teaching that some people would end up in hell, and prayed fervently about it. She finally received this revelation from God: "All will be well, and all will be well, and all manner of thing will be well."

This is a message we also find in your book. At one point, God says to you,

> **"Everyone will succeed because eventually everyone will do the right thing."**

**Jerry:** Even if you spoil your soul, and have other miseries, or make terrible mistakes, you get another opportunity through reincarnation.

**Richard:** There never comes a time when the opportunities are gone. At one point, you asked God about the idea of a final judgment, and God says that there is no *final* judgment. There *is* judgment, but it is implicit in every moment. Every moment can be more or less optimal, every moment is an opportunity for success or failure. And some can fail miserably in this lifetime. But it is never final. There is no final judgment. In the end, "all will be well."

**Jerry:** I was told in that passage that the soul is always judging. We are living here, but we have a soul, an Atman. It is the soul that goes on to the next life, seems to have a stop in Heaven before that, where it has a larger vision of things. Somewhere along the way, you think, "I did the wrong thing in that life." Go back and try it again; that is a learning experience. We watch our children as they grow up and make mistakes. Judgment is the result of experience, and experience is the result of mistakes. That is how you get to good judgment or wisdom.

**Richard:** It reminds me of the movie Groundhog Day. In the movie, the main character wakes up over and over again on the same day until he learns to get that day right. Eventually, he does get it right. In a way, the book is saying something similar. There will always be struggles in life, but these struggles are, finally, enriching and edifying. There is no final failure. There will never come a time when it will all be over. There are infinite possibilities for beauty, truth, goodness, and love, and even our struggles can help us to realize them.

**Jerry:** Yes, and God will be with us in those struggles.

**Richard:** And God will be with us in those struggles, not just as a benign observer, but as an active participant.

**Jerry:** That is a very good final thought, Richard. Thank you for these very rewarding dialogues.

# *References*

Anderson, Sherwood. *Winesburg, Ohio: Text and Criticism*. Penguin Books, 1976.

Aristotle. *The Basic Works of Aristotle*. Edited by Richard McKeon. Translated by W.D. Ross. Random House, 1941.

Augustine. *City of God*. Translated by Henry Bettenson. Penguin Classics, 2004.

Aurobindo, Sri. *The Life Divine*. Lotus Press, 1942.

Ayer, A. J. *Language, Truth, and Logic*. Dover Publications, 1952.

Bohm, David. *Wholeness and the Implicate Order*. Routledge, 2002.

Bradley, F. H. "My Station and Its Duties." In *Ethical Studies*. CreateSpace Independent Publishing Platform, 2017.

Buber, Martin. *I and Thou*. Translated by Walter Kaufmann. Touchstone, 1971.

Clooney, Francis Xavier. *Divine Mother, Blessed Mother: Hindu Goddesses and the Virgin Mary*. Oxford University Press, 2004.

Cracknell, Kenneth. *Justice, Courtesy, and Love: Theologians and Missionaries Encountering World Religions*. Epworth, 1991.

Eck, Diana L. *Encountering God: A Spiritual Journey from Bozeman to Banaras*. Beacon Press, 2014.

Eckhart, Meister. *Meister Eckhart Selected Writings*. Edited and Translated by Oliver Davies. Penguin Books, 1995.

Hegel, G.W. F. *The Phenomenology of Mind*. Translated by J.B. Baillie. Dover Publications, 2003.

Heidegger, Martin. *Being and Time*. Translated by John MacQuarrie and Edward Robinson. Harper & Row, 1962.

Heschel, Abraham Joshua. *God in Search of Man: A Philosophy of Judaism*. Farrar, Straus and Giroux, 1976.

Hick, John. *An Interpretation of Religion: Human Responses to the Transcendent*. Springer, 2004.

Hobbes, Thomas. *Leviathan*. Penguin Classics, 2017.

Huxley, Aldous. *The Perennial Philosophy*. Harper Perennial, 2009.

Jaspers, Karl. *The Origin and Goal of History*. Greenwood Publishing Group, 1976.

Julian of Norwich. *Revelations of Divine Love*. Translated by Barry Windcatt. Oxford University Press, 2015.

Kant, Immanuel. *Critique of Pure Reason*. Edited by James W. Ellington. Translated by Werner S. Pluhar. Hackett Publishing Co., 1996.

## REFERENCES

Kierkegaard, Søren. *The Sickness Unto Death*. Translated by Alastair Hannay. Penguin Classics, 1989.

Lao Tzu. *The Tao Te Ching*. Translated by Stephen Mitchell. Harper Perennial, 1900.

Leibniz, G. W. *Discourse on Metaphysics and The Monadology*. Edited by Albert R. Chandler. Translated by George R. Montgomery. Dover Publications, 2012.

Levenson, Jon Douglas. *The Hebrew Bible, the Old Testament, and Historical Criticism: Jews and Christians in Biblical Studies*. Westminster John Knox Press, 1993.

Martin, Jerry. *God: An Autobiography, As Told to a Philosopher*. Caladium Press, 2016.

Mill, John Stuart. *Utilitarianism*. Hackett Publishing Co., 2002.

Moore, G.E. *Principia Ethica*. Dover Publications, 2004.

Ockham, William. *Philosophical Writings*. Edited and Translated by Philotheus Boehner. Hackett Publishing Co., 1990.

Oxenberg, Richard. *On the Meaning of Human Being: Heidegger and the Bible in Dialogue*. Political Animal Press, 2018.

Race, Alan. *Making Sense of Religious Pluralism*. SPCK Publishing, 2013.

Schuon, Frithjof. *The Transcendent Unity of Religions*. Quest Books, 1984.

Smith, Wilfred Cantwell. *The Meaning and End of Religion*. Fortress Press, 1991.

Teilhard de Chardin, Pierre. *The Phenomenon of Man*. Harper Perennial, 2008.

Tillich, Paul. *Systematic Theology, vols 1, 2, 3*. University of Chicago Press, 1951, 1957, 1963.

Whitehead, Alfred North. *Process and Reality*. Edited and Translated by Philotheus Boehner. Hackett Publishing Co., 1990.

# Index

## A

Abigail 2-6, 12-14, 113, 143, 225
Absolutism 80
Adam and Eve 27, 57, 84, 140-141
Advaita Vedanta 165
Afterlife 115, 120, 148, 191, 234
Agnosticism 4, 12
Aida 47-48, 236
Alexander the Great 99, 134, 147
Allah 127, 175, 208
Amalekites 26, 33
American Academy of Religion (AAR) 46, 128, 217
American Indians 127, 175, 208
Ancient Egyptians 38
Ancient Israel 43, 59, 128, 176
Ancient Scriptures 38, 110, 143
Anderson, Sherwood
  Winesburg, Ohio. 168
Anselm 24
Anthropomorphic 38-40, 53
Aquinas, Thomas 86
Aristotle 9, 62, 68, 182, 232, 245
  Unmoved Mover 75
Arjuna 121, 165
Atheism 12, 85
  Atheistic Secularism 219
Atman 69-70, 111-116, 120-121, 129, 131, 156-159, 228-229, 243
Atman of God 69-70, 113-114, 161, 170, 178
Attachment 164, 167, 189, 223, 233
Aufheben 200
Augustine 14, 84-85, 146, 209
Aurobindo, Sri 107

Avidya. 207
Ayer, A.J. 32

## B

Baptist 7-8, 10, 42-43
Beethoven 119-120
Berkeley 10
Bhagavad Gita 121, 164-165, 223-224
Bible 7, 12, 18, 27, 29-31, 33, 37, 52, 65, 131, 139-140, 196, 227, 229
Biblical God 65, 131
Biblical Theology 23, 196
Big Bang 53-55, 72, 92, 109, 181
Bodhisattva 166-167
Bohm, David 202
Book of Mark 145
Both/And 177
Bradley, Francis Herbert 236
  *My Station and Its Duties* 236
Brahman 67, 70, 112, 114, 129, 152-153, 175-176, 178
Brahman Nirguna 67
Brahman Saguna 67
Buber, Martin 13
Buddha 40, 118, 152, 166-168, 176, 189
Buddhism 43, 46-47, 86, 164, 166-167, 183, 189, 214, 223
  Compassion 213-214
Burton, Richard 61

## C

Caesar, Julius 180
Calvinist 9
Cantwell Smith, Wilfred 129
Caste System 160
Catholicism 9
  Church 154, 197
Chinese Religion 38-39, 162-163
Christianity 24, 137, 143-146, 189, 197, 223-227, 242

Eternal Life  189
  Holy Spirit  240
Christian Orthodoxy  145
Christians as a Sect of the Jews  144
Christian Science  10
Christian Tradition  47, 226, 236
Churchill, Winston  24
Clooney, Francis  227
Comparative Theology  217, 227
Complementalism  222
Confessional Theology  127, 218
Confucianism  155, 163, 212
Confucius  40, 163
Conversion Experience  2
Cosmic Harmony  39, 163, 210
Covenant  29, 59, 128-129, 131, 142
Cracknell, Kenneth.  218
Creation  28, 44, 52-56, 66, 76, 79-81, 88-91, 93, 95, 108, 119, 140, 170-171, 180-183, 198-201, 212
  Doctrines.  52, 145-146, 192
Creator  61, 231
  Ex Nihilo  145

# D

Dalai Lama  214
Dante, Alighieri.  11
Daoism  155, 162, 176
Darwin
  Evolutionary Theory  105
da Vinci, Leonardo  21, 28
Day, Dorothy  43
Death  89, 103, 115, 134, 147, 160, 182-184, 234, 241
De Chardin, Pierre Teilhard  107
Desire  49, 69, 84, 86, 98, 137-138, 184, 187-188, 204-205, 213
Detachment  141, 156-157, 164-165, 189-190
Dharma  121, 160-161, 163, 165-166, 236
Dialectic  33, 35, 39, 135, 182, 187, 225, 233, 238

Conflict and Harmony  237
Desire and Sacrifice  187
Humans and God  39-40, 209
Reading of Scripture  33
Self and Other  225
Truth  35
Dickens, Charles  116
Diversity  29, 30, 42-43, 47-48, 69, 94, 131, 139, 161-162, 172-173, 204, 208, 214-215, 224, 234
  Values  214
Divine Reality  29, 35, 43, 112, 127-128, 131-133, 136, 139, 147, 153, 155, 158, 164, 175, 189-190, 200, 216, 218
Division of Labor  43, 128, 222
Doctrines  23, 143, 146, 227
Dogmatism.  31, 215
Dukkha  189

# E

Eck, Diana  226
Eckhart, Meister.  66, 153
Ego  21, 32, 48-49, 96-98, 102, 165, 185-187, 191, 205-206, 211
  God  100
  Individuated  73, 96
  Separatist  48, 96, 185-186, 206, 211
Either/Or  177, 200
Eliot, Thomas Stearns  11
Emergent God  66-67, 69, 72-77, 79, 81, 88, 99-100, 111, 179
Entropy  183, 188, 198, 241
Equipment  19, 21, 35-36, 48, 155, 172
  Instrument  21-22, 26, 48, 61, 119, 131, 140, 162, 172, 181, 211, 227, 229, 230, 237
Eternal  180, 193
  Damnation  85
  God  39, 62, 179, 183, 198
  Hell  152
  Ideas  92

# INDEX

Peace 187
Reality 69, 179
Thou 13
Truth 148
Eucharist 13
Evangelist 8
Evil 29, 86-87, 91-92, 94, 96-98, 102, 104, 122, 134-135, 138-140, 178, 180, 205-207, 214
   Evil and Suffering 82, 84-86, 88-89, 182-183
   Evil and Suffering Origin 90, 206
   God 29, 85, 99-100, 135, 198
   Overcoming Evil 102, 123, 139, 148
   The Problem of Evil 83-86, 92, 102, 104, 198, 200, 210
Evolutionary Schema 129
Evolving God 38, 40, 58, 107, 111-112, 131, 136, 208, 210, 227, 233
Exclusivism 221
Exodus 33
Exoteric 130-131

## F

Fallibility
Creative Fallibilism 227, 231
Divine 36, 227
Humility 231
Receptor 24, 34, 227
Revelation 28
Feminine God
   Mary, Mother of God 227
   Shechinah 227
Final Judgment 242-243
Fundamental Reality 112, 114, 177

## G

Gandhi, Mahatma 47, 165
Garden of Eden 57, 141, 211
Genesis 27, 33, 51- 55, 61, 140, 145, 192
   New 51-52, 216

*God: An Autobiography, As Told to a Philosopher* 1, 17, 26, 33-34, 51, 83, 86, 100, 105, 124, 126, 139, 145, 147, 154, 157, 160, 163, 166, 173, 179 195-196, 198-199, 207, 213, 215, 221-222, 234
God beyond God. 61-63, 65-73, 75-76, 79-83, 87-89, 91, 93, 95, 98, 102, 111, 113, 115, 125, 159 161, 166, 170-171, 178-183, 187-188, 201, 203, 212
Godhead 63, 66, 153
God of Israel 3, 4, 139
GodSelf
   Individuation 72, 96, 111, 119
God's Loneliness 28, 52, 56, 61, 72-74, 79, 89-90, 93, 98, 102-103 140, 214
Good 31, 52, 62, 86, 91, 122, 136-138, 163, 165, 190, 191, 198, 207, 214, 236
   Ego 48
   God 29, 84, 86, 99, 100, 138, 198, 229
   Judgment 101, 243
Gospel 27, 51, 143-144, 147, 191, 216, 223
Gospel of John 51, 191, 216
Greek New Testament 10
Greek Pantheon 134
   Eros 212

## H

Harmony 1, 3, 47-48, 50, 82, 93, 101, 119, 123, 137-139, 161-163, 169, 171-172, 181-182, 188, 190, 192, 204, 207-208, 210, 212, 229-230, 235-237
Heaven 7-10, 52, 102, 115, 154, 191, 215, 226, 174, 230, 234, 243
Hebrew Bible 27, 29, 139, 227

Hegel, Georg Wilhelm
    Friedrich 57, 200
Heidegger, Martin 97
Hell 9-10, 152, 242
Heschel, Abraham 91
Hick, John 129
Hinduism 43, 66, 70, 111, 112-114,
    127, 129, 143, 153, 156,-157,
    160, 163-164, 167, 178, 189,
    208, 218, 223, 227- 228, 236
Hobbes, Thomas 181
Humanism 11
Huxley, Aldous 130

## I

Identity 78, 113, 163-164
Igbo tribe 218
Illusion 49, 86, 104, 166, 186
Impulse
    Evil 98-99, 206
    Good 98
Incarnation 62, 67, 74-75, 115, 120, 145
Inclusivism 221
Inerrancy 23-24
Infinite World 67, 69, 82, 159
Integration 50, 74, 77-78, 82, 93-94,
    96, 99-101, 136-138, 229-230
Interfaith Dialogue 126, 218
Ishvara 153
Islam 99, 134
I/Thou 6, 13

## J

Jaspers, Karl 40
Jesus 3, 8-9, 14, 25, 27, 40, 71, 102,
    129, 141, 143-148, 156, 168,
    190-191, 197, 226-227, 235
    as Messiah 143
    Cosmic Impact 145
    Cross of Christ 9, 197-198
Judaism. 98, 142, 144, 223-224, 227

Jews and Christianity 144
    Prayer 98
Judas Iscariot 8
Julian of Norwich 122, 242
Justice 85, 132, 204, 228

## K

Kant, Immanuel 203
Karma 117, 160-161, 163
Karuna 213-214
Kierkegaard, Søren 84
Kingdom of God. 147-148, 192
Kingdom of Heaven. 102, 191, 226
Koran 227
Krishna 3, 14, 121, 127, 165, 226

## L

Language 21, 27-28, 53, 56, 140,
    172, 213, 229
Lao Tzu 111, 155
Lawgiver 59, 131, 164, 176, 209-210
Laws of Nature. 80, 86, 183, 188
Lectio Divina 33
Leibniz, Gottfried Wilhelm 107
Levenson, Jon 29
Linear Time 148, 158-159, 179
Lutheran. 127

## M

Mahayana 167
Material Reality 79, 183
Maya 86
Mechanistic Materialism 201-202
Meditation 14, 43, 239
Metaphysical 65, 83, 96, 146, 152, 157,
    167, 171, 186, 197, 203, 234
Methodist 47, 218, 226
Metta 213-214
Michelangelo 79
Moksha 189

## INDEX

Monotheism 99, 133, 135, 138-139
Moore, George Edward 23
Moses 40, 216
Mount Sinai 210
Mysticism 88, 98, 104, 130, 177, 193. 224
Myths
    Finnish 11
    The Bible 140-141

## N

Nagel, Thomas
    *Mind and Cosmos* 202
Napoleon, Bonaparte 97
New Axial Age 40, 129, 222
New Testament 10, 27, 145, 227, 240
Nihilism 80
Nirvana 166, 189
Nothingness 53-54, 61, 72, 89-90, 93, 96, 98, 102-103, 171

## O

Obedience 32, 60, 157, 188, 228
Old Testament 10, 26, 29-30, 37, 99, 147
Oneness 41, 82, 88, 136, 161, 171-172, 180-181, 203-204, 224

## P

Paganism 29, 37, 133
Neo-Pagan 134
Panentheism 200
Pantheism 200
Paradox 39, 55, 84, 95-96, 104, 130, 139, 153, 184
Participatory Nature of God 40, 44, 55, 198, 200, 206, 215, 239
    Participationism 200
Particularity 42, 172-173, 183-185
Pascal's Wager 8
Pentecostal 7-8

People of Israel 29, 38, 59, 128, 131, 141, 209
Perennialism 130
Persian Empire 99
Personal God. 152, 176
Personhood of God 54, 101-102, 108, 152-153, 200
Pharisees 144
Philosophy of Religion 2, 15, 82-83
Physical Reality 164, 189
Physics 59, 72, 153, 202
Plato 9, 32, 68, 92, 182, 207
    Demiurge 92-93
    Eternal Ideas 92
    *Timaeus* 92
    Plotinus 68, 162, 182
Pluralism 221
Polytheism 99, 133-134, 139
Prayer 3, 5, 7, 18, 24-25, 52, 85, 98, 110, 113, 239
Principle of Charity 32-33
Principle of Utility 31
Privation Theory 86
Process Theology 86, 110
Prophet 23, 216
    Abraham. 91, 131-132, 141, 228
    David 141, 147, 202
    Elijah 148, 216
    Isaiah 17-18, 21, 23
    Jeremiah 21, 78, 141, 155
    Mohammed 17-18, 21-22
Psychology 12, 207
Punishment 85, 116, 141
Purgatory 85

## Q

Quantum Physics. 153, 202

## R

Race, Alan 221
*Radically Personal* 234

Ramakrishna, Paramahansa 155
Rationalism 8, 10-11
Reason 31-31, 35, 51, 216
Reductionist 11
Reincarnation 67-68, 115-117, 157, 159, 242
Relativism 214
Replacement Theology 141
Revelation 15, 17-18, 20-23, 26-31, 35-37, 40, 42, 44, 51, 55, 63, 75, 96-99, 104, 122, 124, 126, 128, 132, 134-135 138, 143, 152, 155-156, 166-167, 173-176, 178, 195, 208, 217-218, 227-228, 235, 242
   About Revelations 195
   Buddha. 166
   Diversity 29
   Jesus 191
   Julian of Norwich 122, 242
   Limitations 173, 178
   Revelational Experience 67, 78
   Zoroastrianism 29, 100, 134
Ritualism 133
Rituals 59, 113, 170, 186, 232
Romans 144
Rumi, Jalāl al-Dīn Muhammad 47

## S

Sabbath 192
Sacrifice 49-50, 146, 166, 186-190, 197-198, 211, 228, 232, 237
Sacrificial Love 212-213
Saint Paul 71, 240
Salvation 103, 147-148
Schuon, Frithjof 130
Scientific Revolution 201
Second Noble Truth 189
Self beyond the self 68-69, 95, 111-114, 116, 129, 131, 156
Sermon on the Mount 235
Shakespeare, William 20-21

*Hamlet* 61-62
Shankara, Adi 165-166
Sin 85, 132, 141, 146, 152
Socrates 4, 32, 40, 241
Socratic
   Humility 32, 34-35
   Process 232
   Wisdom 232
Sodom and Gomorrah 131, 228
Spinoza, Baruch 10
Stendhal 85
Stuart-Mill, John 241
Sunyata 183
Supersessionism 142

## T

Talmud 223
Tanha 189
Tao 111, 152, 176
Teleology 201, 203-204, 210-213
Telos 61, 74, 93-94, 108, 119, 219
Temporal 180, 193
   Dimension 103
   God 62, 179
   Perspective 106, 158
   Reality 69, 76, 122, 179
   Worlds 67
Ten Commandments 59-60, 129, 131, 176, 209-210, 212
Thatamanil, John 218
The Great Redactor 27
The Great Spirit 127, 175, 208
Theology Without Walls 41, 127, 217
*Theology Without Walls: The Transreligious Imperative* 219
Tillich, Paul 62
Trinity 143
Truman, Harry 210

# INDEX

## U

Ultimate Reality 61, 66-67, 70, 79, 87, 139, 216, 218
Unheimlichkeit 97-99, 102-103
Union Theological Seminary 218
Unity 42, 47, 73, 87, 90, 93, 98, 162, 181-182, 204-205, 224-225, 230
Upanishads 111, 155

## V

Vedas 227
Vedic Seers 78, 111
Vegetarianism 231
Victory Level 104, 106, 122-123, 192

## W

Western Religions 12, 58, 63, 65, 74-75, 84, 86, 134, 151, 156-157, 164, 177, 207, 226, 234
Wheelwright, Philip
    *The Burning Fountain* 11
Whitehead, Alfred North 107
William of Ockham 24
Won Institute for Buddhist Studies 46

## Y

*Yetzer-Ha-Ra*
    Evil Impulse 98-99
*Yetzer Ha-Tov*
    Good Impulse 98
Yin Yang 163

## Z

Zoroaster 29, 100, 135-136
Zoroastrianism 98-99, 133-134, 137-138

# *Caladium Publishing*

Caladium Publishing was founded in 2015 to address the need for research and exploratory thinking at the boundaries of current spiritual and religious experience.

www.caladiumpublishing.com

CALADIUM PUBLICATIONS

God: An Autobiography, As Told to a Philosopher<br>
by Jerry L. Martin.<br>
www.godanautobiography.com

Jerry Martin was a lifelong agnostic. His naturalistic worldview had no room for God or for a divine dimension of any kind. Yet one day he had occasion to pray. To his surprise, God answered—in words. Being a philosopher, he had a lot of questions… and God had a lot to tell him.

Two Philosophers Wrestle with God: A Dialogue<br>
by Jerry L. Martin and Richard Oxenberg

When Richard Oxenberg read *God: An Autobiography, As told to a Philosopher*, he had many pressing questions about topics covered and contacted the author, Jerry L. Martin. The result was a probing, wide-ranging discussion exploring the nature of the divine and how to live wise and meaningful lives.

## FORTHCOMING PUBLICATIONS

*Theology Without Walls: Founding Essays,*
eds. Christopher Denny and Rita Sherma

*Radically Personal: God and Ourselves in the New Axial Age*
by Jerry L. Martin

*The Sacred / Secular Binary*
*Challenging the Divide in University*
*Culture and Democratic Societies*
By Rory McEntee

*Life Seeking Understanding:*
*How Spiritual But Not Religious and Other Seekers*
*Can Construct Their Own Theology*
By Hans le Grand

*Confessions of a Young Philosopher*
by Abigail L. Rosenthal

# Theology Without Walls

*Theology Without Walls: The Transreligious Imperative* is a collection of essays written by twenty-one scholars making the case for the importance of trans-religious theology.

www.theologywithoutwalls.com

# About the Authors

**DR. JERRY L. MARTIN**
Philosopher and author of the true story, *God: An Autobiography, As Told to A Philosopher*. Jerry has served as the head of the National Endowment for the Humanities and the University of Colorado philosophy department and is the founding chairman of the Theology Without Walls group at the American Academy of Religion and editor of *Theology Without Walls: The Transreligious Imperative*.

Jerry has published on epistemology, philosophy of mind, phenomenology, transreligious theology, and public policy issues. He has a forthcoming book, *Radically Personal: God and Ourselves in the New Axial Age*. Jerry can be contacted at godanautobiography.com

**DR. RICHARD OXENBERG**
Professor at Endicott College with a Ph.D. in Philosophy with a concentration in Ethics and Philosophy of Religion from Emory University. Richard is the author of numerous articles on interreligious theology and the philosophy of spirituality, including his book *On the Meaning of Human Being: Heidegger and the Bible in Dialogue*.

Richard is a contributor to *Theology Without Walls: The Transreligious Imperative*. His works have appeared in the World Council of Faiths' journal, *Interreligious Insight*, as well as *Philosophy Now Magazine*, *Social Philosophy Today*, and others. Richard can be contacted at roxenberg@live.com.

www.ingramcontent.com/pod-product-compliance
Lightning Source LLC
Chambersburg PA
CBHW030432010526
44118CB00011B/611